HANDMADE WEDDINGS

crème fraiche 2023-70
butter 2023-60
lemon meringue 2023-50
sunburst 2023-40

HANDMADE WEDDINGS

MORE THAN 50 CRAFTS TO STYLE *and* PERSONALIZE YOUR BIG DAY

EUNICE MOYLE, SABRINA MOYLE, AND SHANA FAUST

Photographs by JOSEPH DE LEO

CHRONICLE BOOKS
SAN FRANCISCO

EM AND SM: For Mom and Dad and for Daniel and Julian

SF: For Sophie Bea

*

Library of Congress Cataloging-in-Publication Data

Moylc, Eunice.
  Handmade weddings : more than 50 crafts to style and personalize your big day / by Eunice Moyle, Sabrina Moyle, and Shana Faust ; photography by Joseph De Leo ; photo styling by Shana Faust.
    p. cm.
  ISBN 978-0-8118-7450-2
  1. Handicraft. 2. Wedding decorations. I. Moyle, Sabrina. II. Faust, Shana. III. Title.

TT149.M693 2010
745.594'1—dc22

                                                2010008590

Manufactured in China
Illustrations by Eunice Moyle
Design by Kristen Hewitt

10 9 8 7 6 5 4 3 2 1

Chronicle Books LLC
680 Second Street
San Francisco, CA 94107
www.chroniclebooks.com

ACKNOWLEDGMENTS

We are grateful to all of the people who contributed to this book—we couldn't have done it without your talent, patience, and support.

First and foremost are the talented artists and crafters who helped us make, style, and capture each of the projects. Joseph De Leo's flawless eye ensured that each photograph was picture-perfect and each chapter coherent; he was ably assisted by Kazuhito Sakuma and Jesse Brown. Lindsay Milne and Laura Seita from LMD New York created the beautiful floral arrangements. Jayme Murray lent her expertise for creating the book's cover. Tricia Roush contributed the stunning Layered Cockade Ring Pillow (page 183) and helped bring many of the sewing projects to a level of perfection we couldn't have achieved on our own. Chun Yee O'Neill kept us organized on set and helped realize many of the projects; her origami skills are unmatched! Michele Papineau contributed her beautiful calligraphy and know-how for the calligraphy tutorial and created the handwritten stationery featured throughout the book. Finally, our heartfelt thanks to Kim Field, John Ceparano, and Rachel Reese of Aloft Studio, for letting us wreck the place.

Hello!Lucky staff and friends provided untold amounts of support over the year-plus that the projects were in development. We're grateful to the entire Hello!Lucky team for letting our studio become a constant work in progress/den of crafting chaos. Designers Shauna Leytus and Anna Hurley assisted with the graphic design of several of the printed materials, contributed ideas to our brainstorming, and helped execute several craft projects. Renee Grelecki helped organize, pack, and ship a virtual art studio (weighing more than two hundred pounds!) to New York for the photo shoot. Hannah McDevitt contributed her sewing expertise, Francois Vigneault and Shayna Brown lent their extraordinary crafting skills to R & D, and intern Hillary Burgess advised on cupcake-stand ideas. Erin Murphy, Margaret Lee, Jillian Northrup, and Dara Kosberg were our trusty project testers, joining us for many a craft night.

Eunice and Sabrina are also indebted to their clients, particularly Jean and Devin, for providing the inspiration for several of the projects through their own weddings. All of us also owe thanks to the many bloggers, artists, and crafters who provide us with ongoing inspiration—we're honored to be part of such a vibrant wedding and crafting community.

Several companies generously lent us supplies and materials for this book; please see the "Resources" section on page 249 for a full list, as well as for the names of our favorite resources for crafting supplies.

Many thanks to our supporters at Chronicle Books: Kate Woodrow and Jodi Warshaw, who first welcomed our idea; Kristen Hewitt, for her flawless design and boundless enthusiasm; and our editor, Ursula Cary, for coaxing the project to completion.

And finally, such an ambitious project would not have been possible without the support of our family and friends:

EM: Thanks to my husband, Daniel, who *oohs* and *aahs* at the appropriate moments and who, always the gentleman, carried my sewing machine through multiple airports with only the occasional skeptically raised eyebrow.

SM: Thanks to my husband, Julian, for his patience and support, for indulging me with only the occasional wry aside as I wrote or crafted for weeks on end, ignoring other arguably critical responsibilities.

SF: Thanks to my mom, for caring for SB for weeks on end, and to my husband, Steven, for being so loving, supportive, and hilariously funny.

Thank you again to everyone who contributed; you helped make the process of creating this book as delightful as the final product.

CONTENTS

INTRODUCTION

When we first started working on weddings, in 2003, we were awed, inspired, and—let's be honest—a little intimidated by their complexity and their creative possibilities. Eunice and I had recently started our design and letterpress studio, Hello!Lucky, and we were thrilled with the creative opportunities that cards and invitations presented—let alone the myriad other details that coordinate with them to make a wedding day unique.

It was when we met Shana Faust, in 2004, then a senior style editor at *Martha Stewart Weddings*, that the creative potential of a wedding went from an abstract notion to a reality. At the time, Shana was planning her own wedding, and she approached us to help design her stationery. By the time her big day came along, we had collaborated on everything from invitations to place mats, napkin rings, seating cards, favors, drink flags, coasters, and more. No detail was overlooked, and her wedding became one of the most iconic weddings of the year. The experience inspired us to keep creating designs that extend beyond stationery to all the special wedding-day details for a growing number of our clients.

Over the years, we kept in touch with Shana, now a freelance stylist based in New York, and our conversations kept returning to how we might collaborate again. After completing our first craft book, *Handmade Hellos*, in 2008 (a collaboration with some of our favorite independent card artists), our thoughts turned to what we envisioned for our next project: a wedding book that would combine accessible and timeless do-it-yourself (DIY) craft projects with guidance on how to pull all the details together—perhaps one of the most daunting challenges for any bride.

The result is this book, a happy collaboration with our favorite stylist and featuring our unique, collaborative take on ideas that have inspired all of us over the years, with sources ranging from our past clients to magazines, blogs, vintage books, crafters and independent artists, and flea markets.

ABOUT THIS BOOK

Simple, handcrafted details are at the heart of a beautiful wedding. Not only do they give intimacy and charm to the event, but the process of crafting a wedding together with family and friends, detail by detail, makes the big day all the more meaningful—and that much more of a cause for celebration!

That said, it can be hard to know where to begin, what to focus on, and how to pull it all together. There are myriad details to plan, the disparate needs of guests and family members to attend to, and big (read: expensive!) decisions to make. But the creative potential is enormous.

That's why we've pooled our years of experience designing for, crafting, and styling weddings to write this book. In these pages, you'll find a simple approach for breaking down the design of your wedding into manageable, enjoyable steps.

We outline when and how to start, and we detail more than fifty timeless and iconic DIY projects in a variety of wedding styles with simple how-to instructions and practical tips for everything from how much time and money to budget to how to deploy eager helpers. Many of the projects require templates, which you can easily download from www.chroniclebooks.com/handmade-weddings and print out.

In addition, we've scoured our Rolodexes for the very best resources that only the pros know about—from the best party rental companies to unexpected vendors who can produce fantastic wedding details on a budget.

We're excited to share these resources and ideas with you, many of which are wonderful not only for weddings but also for parties, showers, and even decorating your home. A good idea knows no bounds.

We hope that this book helps demystify the process of planning and designing a fabulous event and helps you pull off the wedding of your dreams: a creative and personalized reflection of who you are and a fabulous party for your family and friends.

FINDING INSPIRATION

The first step to planning any wedding is to look for inspiration. Inspiration comes in many forms. The most obvious places to start are wedding magazines and blogs, but be sure to reach for ideas that transcend a traditional wedding aesthetic; these are often the most timeless in the long run.

Start keeping a Web photo album or paper file folder of images that appeal to you. Such images are known as "swipe" in the industry and will be the building blocks for finding your style. Pick out anything that speaks to you, whether it be a wallpaper pattern, a picture frame, a pair of shoes, or a typeface. As you pull your swipe, you'll start developing an idea of what style best reflects you. Most people like a mix of styles, for example, pretty and feminine, with a dash of bohemian.

To organize your thoughts, get a couple of 30-×-40-inch foam-core boards from an art supply store and start printing images you like and pinning or taping them to the board. If you have more than one competing idea or aesthetic, group images onto different boards. You can narrow and edit once you get all your ideas on the wall and see what's working. Keep adding as you find new ideas.

As you look at your ideas, start writing down words that describe what you like (e.g., happy, bold, elegant, whimsical, modern). Articulating your style in words can really help you define and communicate what you like (e.g., "I'm more minimal than girly") to your friends, your spouse-to-be, and your all-important wedding vendors.

Finally, pick the style that will guide your wedding design. Be sure to choose a look that is broad enough to give you sufficient variety to craft the many elements of a wedding.

SOURCES OF INSPIRATION

Restaurants ✶ *Magazines* ✶ Flea markets ✶ *Books* ✶ Product packaging ✶ *Fashion* ✶ Museums ✶ *Farmers' markets* ✶ Hardware stores ✶ *Gardens* ✶ Travel ✶ *Hotels* ✶ Gallerie ✶ *Album covers* ✶ Movies ✶ *Bakeries* ✶ Candy shops ✶ *Graphic design* ✶ Artists ✶ *Fashion designers* ✶ Photographs ✶ *Historical eras* ✶ Everyday things from bygone eras ✶ *Vintage ephemera* ✶ Typefaces ✶ *Architecture* ✶ Patisserie packaging ✶ *Perfume packaging* ✶ Show posters ✶ *Advertisements* ✶ Interior design ✶ *Pottery* ✶ Jewelry design ✶ *Etsy* ✶ Cookbooks ✶ *Retail merchandising displays* ✶ Anthropologie catalogs ✶ *Vintage postcards* ✶ Stamps ✶ *Fabric design* ✶ Scrapbooks ✶ *Family history* ✶ Favorite places and things ✶ *Children's books* ✶ Fairy tales ✶ *Illustration* ✶ Flickr ✶ *Google images* ✶ eBay

SOURCING MATERIALS

As many women know, shopping—for items from groceries to cars—can be a great source of inspiration. The same goes for shopping for craft materials (we like to call it "sourcing"). Sometimes the materials you find will inspire your style, rather than vice versa, and sometimes they will just give you new ideas.

STYLE VERSUS THEME VERSUS MOTIF

One of the most common but avoidable design pitfalls is to confuse a style with a theme or motif. Yet these three design elements, working together, can create a thoughtful, polished look for your big day.

Style

The overall look and feel that guides the design aesthetic (e.g., organic minimal or rustic Americana). Flexible and open to interpretation, style helps bring coherence to the day and can be made up of a variety of distinctive but unified motifs.

Theme

A recurrent idea, event, period, or locale (e.g., *The Great Gatsby*, carnival, beach, nautical). A theme is narrower than a style. Although your style can take cues from or incorporate a theme, it's best to use a theme as a guide, not a gimmick. For example, rather than literally decorating the room with nautical flags, fishing nets, and life preservers, tie your napkins with sailor's knots, or incorporate navy and white stripes into your linens.

Motif

A particular design element that is repeated (e.g., a monogram, a family crest, a silhouette, an icon like the Golden Gate Bridge, or recognizable birds or butterflies). Although a motif can be a wonderful accent through the wedding day, it alone is usually too narrow to guide everything from furniture to décor, and it can get monotonous if repeated too often.

In addition, picking the right materials is the most important factor in determining the outcome of your project, and it trumps skill and crafting technique almost every time. Great materials turn the simplest project into an exquisite detail that will make your guests gasp in delight. Invest a lot of time here—it's worth it, and will ensure that you're happy with your results.

Here are some of our favorite places to source; for more detailed recommendations, see "Resources," page 249. Major urban areas, like New York City and San Francisco, tend to have more resources than smaller towns, so if you happen to be in one of these places while planning your wedding, set aside time to do some sourcing.

ART SUPPLY AND CRAFT STORES

Art supply and craft stores are the first stops in amassing the basic tools and materials you'll need to begin crafting your wedding day. Go to such shops to pick up essentials like a bone folder, cutting mat, glues, punches, and basic papers. For more information on such tools as bone folders, see the appendix "Tools," on page 246.

PAPER STORES

Papers come in all weights, patterns, colors, and sizes. A paper specialty store will have the most extensive and varied collection. Keep an eye out for Japanese paper—the craft of papermaking, and appreciation for design, is well established in Japan, and some of the most exquisite handmade papers and pretty origami patterns come from that country. Also look out for wrapping papers by independent designers, often found at smaller stationery boutiques—these are great raw materials for many craft projects.

CANDY STORES

Candies make great wedding favors, but candy packaging is perhaps even better, as a source of inspiration for design details from place cards to color palettes. An artfully presented DIY candy bar is also a wonderful alternative to a traditional wedding cake.

FABRIC STORES

Fabrics are one of the best sources of pattern and color anywhere because of the sheer variety of both new and vintage styles. Fabrics can be used as inspiration, scanned and printed on paper, or incorporated into everything from pocket squares to ring pillows and fabric-wrapped guest favors. And don't forget to shop the notions section for ribbons, trims, and buttons.

RIBBON OR YARN STORES

Pretty ribbons, and their more unconventional cousins, yarns, are essential for adding the finishing touch to many wedding-day details. Satin and grosgrain are classic, elegant, and available in just about any color. That said, be sure to look out for more quirky or unexpected choices like minimal jute yarns, graphic striped baker's twine, or vintage velvets.

HARDWARE AND GARDEN STORES

Hardware and garden stores are full of useful supplies that can be adapted to craft projects. Look for items like wood for making signs, spray paint, decorative hooks, number stencils, twine, wire, and utilitarian vessels or shades that can be covered with paper or fabric, transforming them into a pretty centerpiece or decorative lamp shade.

HOME DÉCOR STORES

Affordable housewares stores are perfect places to look for a vase for a guest-book table, accent cushions for a lounge, or trays or vases for centerpieces.

Be aware of what you can rent, as opposed to having to buy, and keep in mind how items could be reused after the wedding.

FLORAL SUPPLY STORES

Most major cities have a flower market that serves industry professionals but that is open to the general public at set times during the week. Visit these for both a basic education in different types of flowers as well as everything from millinery items (silk butterflies, birds' nests, and the like) to wreath forms, ribbons, floral tape and twine, and basic vessels that can be used for centerpieces.

RESTAURANT AND BAKING SUPPLY STORES

Restaurant and baking supply stores are a treasure trove for entertaining. Look for simple table-number and place-card stands, which can be spray painted, as well as colorful cupcake cups, cake boards, baker's twine, and all manner of food packaging, from favor or pastry boxes to tags, labels, and glassine sleeves. Remember, however, that many food-service items can be rented, so concentrate on sourcing craft materials, disposable items, or items you plan to embellish.

PARTY SUPPLY OR IMPORT STORES

Although most party supplies are too kitschy for weddings, party supply stores do offer a few gems such as mini maracas, kazoos, and festive blow-outs that can make fun, tasteful additions to a wedding. Look out for crepe paper for crafting, paper streamers, tissue paper balls, and paper lanterns. Asian import stores are a great resource for lanterns, tea tins, soaps, and fans.

FLEA MARKETS AND VINTAGE STORES

Flea markets and vintage stores are perhaps our favorite places to go for inspiration. Vintage items—from handkerchiefs and ribbons to baskets and bottles—are wonderful, unique accents for any wedding and a perfect complement to handcrafted details. Keep an eye out for vintage stamps, which are a lovely embellishment to any invitation, as well as items like wooden letters; frames; vases, jars, and bottles for centerpieces; and baskets, trays, and buckets for presenting programs, favors, parasols, and the like.

FONT STORES

Online stores, such as www.myfonts.com, offer a huge array of fonts; download one or two distinctive styles, and use them to tie all your printed materials together. Most sites allow you to search by style and preview sample text (so you can see how you and your fiancé's name will look, for example). Fonts generally cost $20 to $60, but some are free.

Installing a font can be as simple as downloading the file and dragging it to your Fonts folder, though the process varies depending on your type of computer (Mac or PC) and your operating system (e.g., Windows NT, Mac OS X, etc.).

Fonts come in a variety of formats that work with different computers and operating systems. All of the fonts used in this book are OpenType fonts (file names ending in .otf), which are compatible with both PCs and Macs.

All templates with customizable text used in this book (available at www.chroniclebooks.com/handmade-weddings) require that you own specific fonts, and the finished project will not look right without them. When a specific font is required, it is listed in the Tools section at the beginning of each project. Before purchasing, be sure you are downloading the right version of the font, and make sure that the font name matches exactly the font listed in the project.

If you are having trouble downloading fonts, you can search online for instructions (using the search term "installing OpenType fonts on PC," for example). Graphic design and software user forums, the Web site for your operating system, or the Web site where you purchased your fonts can all provide specific instructions for your computer and operating system, if needed.

ELEMENTS OF A HANDMADE WEDDING

Many elements go into designing a wedding, from essentials to special extras. Although just about every aspect of a wedding has DIY potential, your schedule, budget, and energy will limit the number of projects you can take on. It's therefore ideal to think about which items are the most high-impact and feasible to make in the time you have—and important to you in terms of adding a personal, creative touch to your wedding.

Here is a quick framework that can help you think about which ideas to prioritize.

Definitely DIY	Buy, rent, or plan ahead
One-offs, e.g., a ring pillow	Multiples, e.g., invitations
Simple projects	Complicated projects, or those that require learning a new skill
Projects that play to an existing creative talent, skill, or hobby, e.g., knitting, sewing, or collecting	Anything that could affect guest comfort or safety, e.g., furniture or food
Items that have sentimental or keepsake value	Anything that is cheaper to buy or rent or that you just don't feel like making

On the following page we've provided a checklist of elements that make up a typical wedding. Although all of them have DIY potential, we've found that the items in bold type generally are the easiest to tackle. Remember, DIY projects are usually more time-consuming, and can sometimes be more expensive, than hiring a pro or buying a premade item. So choose wisely, and don't put too much pressure on yourself. The goal is to be healthy, happy, and relaxed on your wedding day, so enlist lots of help and keep your expectations grounded.

CHECKLIST

Invitations
- ○ Save-the-dates
- ○ Wedding invitations and enclosures
- ○ Rehearsal dinner invitations
- ○ Thank-you notes

Favors and gifts
- ○ Guest welcome bag or letter
- ○ Favors
- ○ Bridesmaids and groomsmen gifts

Attire
- ○ Corsages (for bridesmaids, mothers of the bride and groom)
- ○ Boutonnieres (for groomsmen, fathers of the bride and groom)
- ○ Flower girl garland, headband, or tiara/crown
- ○ Bridal headpiece or veil
- ○ Neckties, bow ties, pocket squares, and cuff links (for groomsmen)
- ○ Bride and bridesmaids jewelry
- ○ Bridal party attire

Ceremony
- ○ Welcome sign
- ○ Programs
- ○ Altar or chuppah
- ○ Aisle markers
- ○ Reserved seating signs
- ○ Ring pillow
- ○ Flower girl basket or apron
- ○ Confetti pouches

Reception—cocktail hour
- ○ Seating cards/displays
- ○ Drink flags or stir sticks
- ○ Food packaging (e.g., doughnut bags, paper cones)
- ○ Cocktail napkins
- ○ Bar and buffet signs
- ○ Photo booth or photo-booth backdrop
- ○ Guest book

Reception—dinner and dancing
- ○ Pom-poms or garlands
- ○ Table runners
- ○ Centerpieces
- ○ Votives or decorative vessels for flowers
- ○ Table numbers
- ○ Place settings and napkins
- ○ Menus
- ○ Place cards
- ○ Bride and groom's seating signs
- ○ Cake topper
- ○ Cake or dessert bar stands
- ○ Just Married sign

HOW TO USE THIS BOOK

This book is divided into six chapters, each featuring a different wedding style. Each style is broken down to its basic elements followed by simple ideas for pulling the look together, and eight to ten DIY projects. Our goal is to help you understand the vocabulary of a style, visualize how it can be carried throughout your entire wedding, and realize that vision. Keep in mind that the styles we've chosen to highlight are just a taste of what's possible (believe us, it was tough to narrow them down to just six!). Each look can be made your own simply by choosing different colors, patterns, typefaces, or materials.

The projects within each chapter cover the gamut of wedding details, ranging from invitations to attire to décor. Because most of the projects can be adapted to a variety of wedding venues, times of year, themes, and seasons, we have also suggested ideas for variations at the end of each.

At the beginning of each project, you'll find the following handy key for helping you plan ahead, budget, and prepare to craft:

LEVEL
Easy

. . . .

CATEGORY
Décor

. . . .

TIME
6 to 7 hours for
five 6-ft. strands

. . . .

WHEN TO START
4 to 6 weeks before
the wedding

. . . .

**GROUP OR
INDIVIDUAL**
Individual, or
a small group

. . . .

BUDGET
$50 to $100, depending
on fabrics chosen

LEVEL, OR LEVEL OF DIFFICULTY

- Easy. Requires little or no crafting experience—just the ability to follow instructions and use simple tools like scissors, paper punches, or a craft knife.
- Moderate. Takes a bit of artistic or crafting skill or at least patience and attention to detail. May also involve a more complicated series of steps.
- Advanced. Typically requires previous experience in a particular craft, such as sewing or printmaking. Often entails a lot of steps, some problem solving, and patience!

CATEGORY

The part of the wedding to which the project belongs.
- Invitations: wedding invitations, save-the-dates, thank-you notes
- Décor: pom-poms and garlands, signs—can be used at the ceremony, reception, or at showers or the rehearsal dinner
- Attire: boutonnieres and corsages, groomsmen's attire, bridesmaids' attire, flower girl's attire
- Ceremony: programs, ring pillows
- Reception: centerpieces, menus, place cards, seating cards, table numbers
- Favors and gifts: guest favors, welcome bags, bridal party gifts, guest book

TIME

The rough amount of time it takes to complete the project. Typically, this is estimated assuming that you follow our suggestions regarding making the project in a group or individually.

WHEN TO START

Our suggested time line for when to start the project. Circumstances vary from wedding to wedding, so keep the following in mind as you plan your schedule:

Projects to start early

• Complicated or labor-intensive
• Need to make en masse
• Not dependent on information that is not yet available, such as number of tables, reception hall measurements, or final guest count
• Not perishable

Projects to start closer to your wedding

• Simple
• Need only a few items
• Require last-minute information, such as final guest count, menu, or program
• Perishable or might get damaged if stored for a long time

It can be helpful to literally schedule each project into your calendar, with reminders in advance for decisions that need to be made to get started (e.g., confirm the menu with the caterer, order bridesmaids' dresses, confirm final guest count, etc.).

GROUP OR INDIVIDUAL

Here we've offered suggestions for whether the project is most efficiently tackled on your own or with the help of friends. Where a group is the best approach, we've broken the project down into stations that you can set up in advance to create a mini assembly line—this makes crafting projects go a lot more quickly, so you can have more fun while you're at it!

BUDGET

The rough cost of making the project. The budget usually assumes that you have most of the basic crafting tools called for in the project, such as a craft knife and cutting mat, laser or inkjet printer, or sewing machine. It mainly includes materials that are unique to the project (and will be consumed by it), and it reflects the cost of making the number of multiples identified at the beginning of the project instructions. Adjust the budget if you'll be buying any of the tools required for the first time in order to get started. Also note that material costs may vary by region and may be higher if you are ordering supplies online and paying for shipping.

The project key is followed by a list of materials and tools you'll need to complete the project. These include any templates that are needed, available at www.chroniclebooks.com/handmade-weddings.

Finally, in the Appendixes (page 246) you'll find more handy information, such as a wedding planning time line and checklist, instructions for how to address and mail your invitations, and a list of resources.

CRAFTING TIPS

And finally, a few words to the wise to make your crafting go more efficiently:

1. Start with a prototype. A project doesn't always work perfectly right out of the gate, so budget some time and extra materials for making a prototype first. This is especially true if you are inviting a group of friends over to crank out dozens of an item. Not all materials are created equally, so always test to make sure that the ones you've chosen behave the way you expect them to. For example, does your rubber-stamp ink bleed when stamped on your paper? (If so, the paper is too absorbent—try a different paper, or rub over the area to be stamped with a white pencil.) Does the card stock you purchased for your invitations feed through your printer?

2. Take your time. Haste makes waste, particularly when it comes to crafting materials, which can be expensive. Always take the time to double check your measurements (measure twice, cut once!). The key to a beautiful DIY wedding element is that it looks handmade yet also polished and refined. Work at a leisurely pace, paying attention to details, so that your project looks its best and is an accurate reflection of the time and energy that went into it.

3. Have fun! Crafting is a wonderful escape from the mundane and abstract goings-on of day-to-day life. There's simply nothing like making a beautiful object from scratch and seeing the tangible results of your efforts. Savor the experience, and share it with your friends!

RETRO HOMESPUN

SWEET, RUSTIC, CHARMING, AND HANDMADE, retro homespun details
are all about nostalgia for the crafts and comfort of a bygone era. Whether it be quilting,
knitting, or embroidery, these techniques and textures instantly bring a cozy,
heirloom quality to a modern wedding.

RETRO HOMESPUN STYLE

PALETTES

Cherry

Tangerine

Butter yellow

Coral

Bluebell

INSPIRATION
Cath Kidston, Liberty of London, vintage fabrics and wallpapers

FONTS
P22 Declaration Script, Nelly Script, Emily Austin, Rosewood Fill, Filosofia
Neutra Book, Bryant Regular

TEXTURES
Cotton fabric, stitching, embroidery, cross-stitch, buttons, gingham,
polka dots, vintage florals, quilting, clothespins, twill tape, etched glass,
enameled aluminum, eyelet lace, stripes, plaids

VENUES
Backyard, ranch, barn, farm, winery, historic home, rustic hotel

DETAILS
Make your getaway in a vintage car or on a tandem bicycle ✻ *Serve traditional comfort food family style—spaghetti and meatballs, mac and cheese, pork chops, apple sauce, and mashed potatoes* ✻ For appetizers or parting treats, serve nostalgic favorites like lemonade, cracker jacks, doughnut holes, or milk and cookies ✻ *Hang seating cards using clothespins attached to string or pretty ribbon* ✻ Create your own photo booth, with retro fabric as a backdrop ✻ *Hand out parasols for a sunny-day wedding*

PUTTING IT ALL TOGETHER

1.

WILDFLOWERS
Choose wildflowers such as lilacs and sweet peas (spring), Queen Anne's lace and daisies (summer), sunflowers and zinnias (fall), and jasmine and forget-me-nots (winter).

2.

MASON JARS, MILK GLASS, AND TEA TINS
These are perfect vessels for flowers, and can also be filled with dried beans or pebbles to hold votive candles.

3.

MIX-AND-MATCH PLATES OR NAPKINS
Collect vintage plates from flea markets, eBay, and Goodwill. Or, rent simple white plates and sew mix-and-match patterned napkins.

4.

VINTAGE HANKIES
Hand these out to guests to dry their eyes during the ceremony.

5.

HOMEMADE PIES
Serve an assortment of pies instead of cake (a small cutting cake can used for a photo opportunity). Make pie flags noting the different flavors out of patterned paper and a toothpick.

RETRO HOMESPUN INVITATIONS

This invitation combines a simple design with lovely handmade details: a twine and button tie, rounded corners, and coordinating envelope liners. Experiment with a variety of different types of buttons and twine, giving each invitation its own unique personality.

LEVEL
Easy

CATEGORY
Invitations

TIME
Printing—4 hours
Assembly—4 hours

WHEN TO START
12 weeks before the wedding (Invitations should be mailed 8 weeks before the wedding.)

GROUP OR INDIVIDUAL
Group (after printing)

- *Station 1: Trim the pieces.*
- *Station 2: Round the corners.*
- *Station 3: Cut out envelope liners.*
- *Station 4: Line the envelopes.*
- *Station 5: Affix RSVP labels, stamps, and guest labels (once the envelopes have been lined).*
- *Station 6: Collate the invitations and the RSVP cards and add button and band.*
- *Station 7: Stuff and seal the envelopes.*

BUDGET
$250 (excluding postage)

MATERIALS
Makes 100 invitations
- Sixty 8 1/2-×-11-inch sheets ecru or white card stock for invitations
- Forty 8 1/2-×-11-inch sheets ecru or white card stock for RSVP cards
- One hundred twenty-five 8 1/2-×-11-inch sheets ecru or white text-weight paper for envelope liners
- Twenty 8 1/2-×-11-inch sheets ecru or white label stock for guest labels
- Fifteen 8 1/2-×-11 inch sheets ecru or white label stock for return labels
- One hundred 4-bar envelopes
- One hundred ten A7 envelopes
- 100 yards twine
- One hundred 1/2-inch buttons
- Postage stamps for RSVP card and invitation envelopes (Note that because of the button, the invitation will be subject to a non-machinable surcharge.

Check with your post office or online, at www.usps.com, for rates.)

TOOLS
- Retro Homespun Invitation and envelope liner templates (available online at www.chroniclebooks.com/handmade-weddings)
- Fonts: Bryant Regular and P22 Declaration Script
- Inkjet printer, with extra cartridges
- Craft knife, with extra blades, or a paper cutter
- Ruler
- Cutting mat
- Corner rounder (optional)
- Bone folder
- Glue sticks
- Scissors

Note: If you are assembling invitations with a group, be sure to have enough craft knives, rulers, cutting mats, and glue sticks to keep everyone busy—we recommend four of each.

HOW TO

1. Customize and print your invitations, labels, and envelope liner paper.

Customize your invitation, reply card, and labels text using the online templates and print the pieces on an inkjet printer. For the two-sided RSVP card, be sure to check the front-to-back alignment before printing all. Print out your envelope liner paper usine the online template.

2. Cut out your invitations and labels.

Using a craft knife, ruler, and cutting mat or a paper cutter, cut the invitations, reply cards, and labels along the crop marks provided. If using a craft knife, as soon as your blade begins to dull, put in a fresh blade.

Optionally, round the corners of all pieces using a corner rounder.

Tip: While most craft stores sell inexpensive corner rounding punches, these can be hard to use when making multiple invitations. Consider investing in a tabletop corner rounder such as those made by Lassco.

3. Line the envelopes.

Using the templates provided, cut out the envelope liners using a craft knife and ruler. If the template does not fit your envelopes, you can make your own: trace the outline of an open envelope onto a piece of card stock or cardboard. Cut it out with a craft knife, trace the shape onto your envelope liner paper, and cut out.

Using a ruler and bone folder, score each liner as indicated on the template. To line the envelopes, insert the liner into an envelope. Fold the triangular part of the liner down, aligning the fold with the crease in the envelope flap. Spread glue over the folded area. Fold the envelope flap down over the glued portion of the liner. Press firmly. Open the envelope and let dry.

4. Assemble the invitations.

Affix the RSVP labels to the 4-bar envelopes, and affix the guest labels to the A7 envelopes. Remember to leave at least $1/4$ inch clear at the bottom of each envelope for post office bar coding. Affix postage to the RSVP and invitation envelopes. Collate the invitation and RSVP cards, and wrap each set with a button and string. Cut a 30- to 36-inch piece of string for each invitation. Wrap the string around the invitation lengthwise from front to back, cross over and wrap crosswise from back to front. Thread each end of the string through a buttonhole and tie in a bow. Insert each invitation set into an envelope so that when it is pulled out with your right hand, the invitation is facing the right way up. Seal the envelopes with a glue stick.

CUPCAKE LINER POM-POMS

LEVEL
Easy

CATEGORY
Décor

TIME
4 to 6 hours

WHEN TO START
8 to 10 weeks before
the wedding

**GROUP OR
INDIVIDUAL**
Group

- *Station 1: Flatten and fold the
cupcake liners.*
- *Station 2: Make the pom-poms.*
- *Station 3: Attach the pom-poms
to the string.*

BUDGET
$50 to $75

Pretty patterned cupcake liners become festive pom-pom strands with a bit of glue and string. Hang these over your reception tables or in your cocktail area, and feel free to mix and match colors and patterns within your palette.

MATERIALS
Makes six 12-foot strands
- 720 cupcake liners, approximately 120 per strand
- Six 12-foot lengths white kitchen string

TOOLS
- Bone folder
- Rubber bands (optional)
- Glue sticks
- Clear tape

HOW TO
1. Flatten and fold your cupcake liners.

Using a bone folder, flatten each cupcake liner into a circle. Fold in half, wrong-side out. Repeat for all of your liners. You will need 10 identical liners per pom-pom. If you are using a variety of patterns and colors, stack or rubber band them by pattern. If your cupcake liners have scalloped edges, be sure to fold them along the same axis every time. This will ensure that the segments that make up each pom-pom are all symmetrical, making for a pleasing whole.

2. Make the pom-poms.

Place 10 folded cupcake liners, of the same pattern and color, on your work surface. Using a glue stick, spread glue over one half of a cupcake liner. Align it to the corresponding half of a second cupcake liner. Press down and smooth with your bone folder *(figure 1, page 29)*. Let dry. Continue attaching the cupcake liner halves, smoothing each segment as you go to ensure a secure bond. Do not glue the last segment. When complete, the pom-pom will form an accordion-like

sphere with one open segment, which allows you to flatten the pom-pom into a circle (*figure 2*). Let dry completely. Continue making pom-poms.

3. Attach the pom-poms to the string.

Leaving about 2 feet on either end of the garland for hanging, attach the pom-poms along the string, at 2-inch intervals (or greater if desired). To attach, lay a flattened pom-pom on your work surface and align the string along its central axis (i.e., along the crease). Secure the string with two small pieces of clear tape, one on each end of the pom-pom. Spread glue over one half of the circle, as well as on the string, and sandwich the two halves of the open segment together, trapping the string (*figure 3*). Let dry. When all the pom-poms are attached and dry, hang the garland. "Fluff" the pom-pom segments by hand to create full circles.

VARIATIONS

- **Happy Graphic:** Choose cupcake liners in bright solid colors. In lieu of white kitchen string, use a colorful string or cord.

- **Found:** Use a variety of patterned and solid liners in blues, reds, greens, and yellows. In lieu of white kitchen string, consider using red and white striped baker's twine or jute.

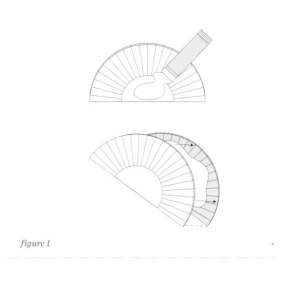

figure 1

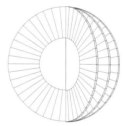

figure 2

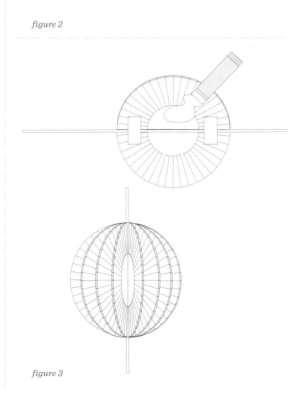

figure 3

YARN-WRAPPED BOTTLES

LEVEL
Easy

CATEGORY
Décor

TIME
4 to 6 hours

WHEN TO START
3 to 4 weeks before
the wedding

**GROUP OR
INDIVIDUAL**
Group; have each
person work
on wrapping
2 to 4 bottles.

BUDGET
$20 to $30

A bit of yarn in your color palette transforms plain glass bottles and jars into pretty accent pieces. Start with vintage milk bottles or recycled jam jars, or pick up some Ball jars in clear or blue shades. Coil yarn around all or some of the jar, or experiment with adding a bow. Avoid round jars or vases: although a slight curve or a tapered bottleneck is not too difficult to cover, a fishbowl shape can be tricky.

MATERIALS
Makes 12 jars
- 12 glass jars or bottles (we recommend milk bottles or Ball jars in different sizes)
- 1 to 3 skeins yarn in complementary colors (go with chunky yarn for a more homespun look)

TOOLS
- Double-sided tape
- Scissors

HOW TO

1. Apply tape to curved areas.
Apply double-sided tape evenly over any curved portions of the bottle that you'd like to cover with yarn, such as the curved neck of the milk bottle; this will hold the yarn in place, making an easier job of wrapping as well as a neater-looking result.

2. Wrap the bottle.
Starting with the lip or base of the bottle, attach the end of your yarn to the bottle with a small piece of double-sided tape, slightly below (if starting from the lip) or above (if starting from the base) where you want the yarn coil to begin. Begin wrapping the yarn around the bottle, wrapping over the loose end and making tight, even coils that follow the profile of the bottle (*figure 1, page 32*). When you are about 1/2 inch from where you want to stop wrapping, apply

a small piece of double-sided tape to your intended stopping point, wrap to there, trim the yarn, and smooth the loose end down onto the tape to hide it.

3. Add a bow (optional).

To add a bow, begin wrapping from the base of the bottle (or wherever you want the yarn coils to begin). When you reach the spot where you would like to place your bow, apply a bit of double-sided tape to that spot and press the yarn down to secure it. Measure about 10 inches of yarn, and then trim it so that the end hangs loose. This will be the first half of your bow. Starting with a new piece of yarn, begin wrapping from the lip of the bottle. Stop when you reach the first half of your bow. Apply a bit of double-sided tape just to the right of it, and press the yarn down to secure. Measure about 10 inches of yarn, and trim. This will be the second half of your bow. Tie the two loose ends together in a bow. Trim the ends with scissors.

VARIATIONS

- **Happy Graphic:** Use fat yarn in red and other primary colors.

- **Organic Minimal:** Use thin yarns in whites, grays, sea foam, or khaki. Wrap the bottles in an arbitrary crisscross pattern to create an organic, Japanese-inspired look.

figure 1

EMBROIDERY WELCOME HOOP

4

LEVEL
Moderate

CATEGORY
Décor

TIME
30 to 40 hours per large, elaborate hoop; 4 to 5 hours per small, simple hoop

WHEN TO START
6 to 12 months before the wedding

GROUP OR INDIVIDUAL
Individual

BUDGET
Less than $50

Hung at the entrance to the ceremony site or reception hall, these charming embroidery hoops also make simple, permanent keepsakes. Because embroidery is simple but time-consuming, get started early, as soon as you have your venue and color palette. For busy brides, this project is portable: once you master the basic stitches, you can take it almost anywhere—on a plane, on a bus, to the beach, or to your sofa.

MATERIALS
Makes 1 hoop

For the large "Welcome" hoop:
- 20-×-30-inch piece embroidery fabric with a visible weave, also known as Aida
- 14-inch wood quilting hoop
- 6-thread embroidery floss in eight to ten colors (we used one skein each of charcoal, orange, dark coral, light coral, dark green, light green, yellow, dark blue, light blue, and red)

For the small monogram hoop:
- 15-×-15-inch piece of medium-weight fabric
- 12-inch wood quilting hoop
- 6-thread embroidery floss in two colors (we used one skein each of charcoal and red)
- 1-inch ribbon for hanging (optional)

TOOLS
- Embroidery Welcome Hoop templates (available online at www.chroniclebooks.com/handmade-weddings)
- Font: Nelly Script
- Transfer paper (available at art supply stores)
- Embroidery needle
- Scissors
- Thumbtacks or hot glue (optional)

HOW TO

1. Set up your hoop and template.

Transfer the Embroidery Welcome Hoop template onto the fabric. To transfer onto porous fabric, lay the fabric directly over the template and trace. To transfer the pattern onto thicker fabric, lay the transfer paper carbon-side down over the fabric and place the template right-side

up, on top of it. Trace over the template with a pencil (or anything that applies pressure)—the lines will be transferred to the fabric. Mount the fabric in the hoop, pulling it taut on all sides.

2. Stitch the design.

Beginning with the more neutral elements of your design (e.g., leaves, letters), stitch the pattern. Thread the needle with the desired color, and tie a knot at one end. Most stitches will require that you leave the embroidery floss exactly as it comes off the skein. For more delicate stitches, divide the strands in half, using three strands instead of six.

SIMPLE STITCHES

Running (or straight) stitch. Creates a dashed line. Great for making stems, lines, or letters.

Bring your needle up through the fabric at your starting point. Pierce the needle back through the fabric to create the first stitch. Repeat, keeping the length of the stitches even *(figure 1)*.

Backstitch. Creates a continuous line, as each stitch slightly overlaps with the previous one. Great for making stems, lines, or letters.

Bring your needle up through the fabric at your starting point. Make a straight stitch, piercing the needle back down through the fabric about 1/4 inch from your starting point to create the first stitch. Bring the needle back up through the previous stitch, about 1/16 inch from where it ended. Make another straight stitch *(figure 2)*.

Satin stitch. Creates a filled-in effect. Great for "coloring in" flower petals and leaves.

Starting at one end of your shape, make a series of straight stitches, keeping each stitch adjacent to the last to create a solid area of color and adjusting the end points to meet the outline of the shape. Be

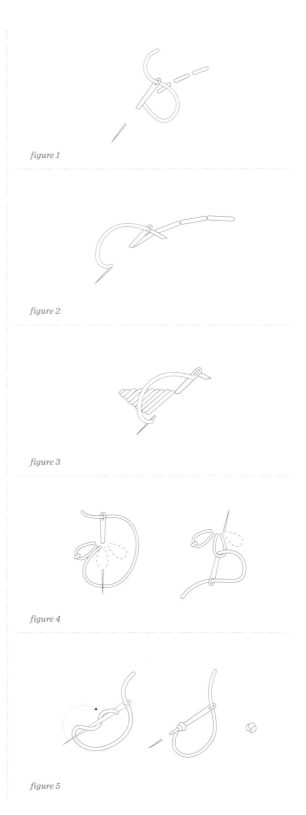

figure 1

figure 2

figure 3

figure 4

figure 5

sure to put your needle in outside the outline of the shape to prevent the marks from showing *(figure 3, page 35)*.

Detached chain stitch. Creates an open loop that is anchored by a small stitch on one end. Great for making small leaves.

Bring your needle up through the fabric at the starting point, typically the base of your leaf. Make a small straight stitch, piercing the needle back down through the fabric at the base of the leaf, close to the starting point (don't go back through the starting point, as the thread will pull through). Keeping the thread loose, slowly pull to create a loop about 1/2 inch in diameter. Hold the end of this loop down with your right thumb where you would like the leaf shape to end. Bring the needle back up at this point, and make another small straight stitch to anchor the loop down. Pull taut *(figure 4, page 35)*.

French knot. Creates a small knot. Great for filling in flower centers and adding texture to your design.

Bring your needle up through the fabric at your starting point. Catch the floss on your needle and wrap it around the needle twice, holding the floss taut. Point the needle through the knot and push into the fabric close to the starting point, pulling the knot tight as you go *(figure 5, page 35)*.

3. Finish the hoop.

Trim the fabric around the underside edges of the hoop. If desired, affix a length of coordinating 1-inch ribbon for hanging to the inside of the hoop, using small thumbtacks or hot glue. The hoop will also hang easily on a nail on its own.

VARIATIONS

Just about any design or phrase you can think of can be embroidered. To give the hoop a more graphic look, consider spray painting or staining it.

• **Happy Graphic:** Stitch the monogram into a bold solid fabric or a graphic pattern, such as a stripe or polka dot.

• **Organic Minimal:** Use burlap as your base, and choose neutral embroidery threads. Consider creating your own design, inspired by such artists as Lotta Jansdotter, Jill Bliss, or Hable Construction.

• **Modern Classic:** Find a classic-looking font (Bickham, Lucia, or Mrs. Eaves) from www.myfonts.com (fonts for sale), www.dafont.com (free fonts), or other font Web sites. Type your initials, and print them out using a laser or inkjet printer. Transfer onto your embroidery fabric. Create two hoops, each with the bride's and groom's initials or silhouettes. Spray paint the hoops black, white, or another color in your palette.

MIX-&-MATCH POCKET SQUARES

LEVEL
Easy

CATEGORY
Attire

TIME
2 hours

WHEN TO START
4 to 8 weeks before
the wedding

**GROUP OR
INDIVIDUAL**
Individual

BUDGET
$5 to $10 per pocket square,
depending on fabric cost

Homemade pocket squares are a great way to give a personal touch to your groomsmen's attire, and they make lovely keepsakes. Add flair with a contrasting stitch, buttons, rickrack trim, or fringe. Be sure to choose patterns that are the right scale (e.g., not too big) and not too girly!

MATERIALS

Makes 1 pocket square

- 1/2 yard cotton fabric, washed (will make three pocket squares)
- Matching thread
- Dritz Fray Check (or something similar, available at Jo-Ann Fabrics, at www.joann.com; optional)
- Rickrack trim (optional)
- Contrasting thread (optional)
- Embroidery floss (optional)
- 3 buttons (optional)

TOOLS

- Iron and ironing board
- Scissors
- Ruler (we recommend a clear, gridded quilting ruler, such as OmniGrid)
- Cutting mat
- Rotary cutter
- Sewing needle
- Clover Chaco Liner (A chalk-dispensing pen with easily removeable chalk. Optional for fringed edge, contrast stitch, and button variations; available from www.clotilde.com.)
- Straight pins (optional)
- Long, slender embroidery needle (optional)

HOW TO

1. Cut your fabric.

Iron your washed fabric and trim off any selvedge, the self-finished edges of fabric. Using your ruler, cutting mat, and rotary cutter, cut a 12 1/2-×-12 1/2-inch square. Cut a straight bottom and side edge. Fold in half on the diagonal to form a triangle that is 12 1/2 inches long on either side. Trim the remaining two sides of the square.

2. Roll the edge.

With the fabric facing wrong-side up, roll the edge of the fabric tightly toward you between your thumb and forefinger. Roll approximately 1/4 inch of the fabric (we rolled the edge twice).

3. Sew the hem.

Thread your needle and tie a knot. Place the needle into the end of the rolled edge and come out about 1/2 inch away just along the bottom of your rolled edge. Pull the needle through. Catch approximately 1/16 inch of the body of the hand-kerchief along the edge where the roll meets the fabric. Pull the needle through. Insert the needle back into the roll to the left of where you last came out. Run the needle through the roll for approximately 1/2 inch. Bring the needle back out of the roll and again catch about 1/16 inch of the body fabric (*figure 1*). Continue along the entire length of one side of your pocket square. When you come to the end of the side, bring the needle through the roll and tie off with a small knot (this way the knot will end up tucked neatly into the roll). Roll and stitch the opposite side of the handkerchief and then the remaining two sides, rolling tightly to make neat edges.

4. Jazz it up.

Add rickrack trim: Make a simple rolled hem: Cut a neat edge on one end of the rickrack, and treat the edge with a small amount of Fray Check and let dry. Thread a needle with thread that matches the trim you've chosen. Starting near the center of one of the straight sides of the fabric (not on a corner), lay one end of the trim on the edge of the fabric, centering the trim lengthwise on the rolled hem. Leaving a 1-inch tail of trim loose at the end, sew the trim to the rolled hem with short, even 1/8-inch running stitches (see page 35). Run the needle through the center of the rolled hem between each stitch, so the stitch doesn't show on the other side. As you curve your stitching to fit

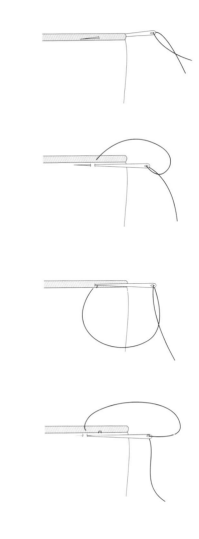

figure 1

around the corners, keep the thread fairly loose or the fabric will pucker and will not lay flat. When you have sewn to 2 inches from where you started, line the two ends up and decide where would be the best place to cut each for a smooth-looking join. Cut one side 1/4 inch longer than the other so the ends overlap. Apply a small amount of Fray Check to both cut edges and let dry. Finish sewing the loose ends down, one side and then the other, overlapping them.

Fringe the edges: Use two contrasting medium-weight linens or woven fabrics. Cut two 12 1/2-inch squares carefully along the grain. Using fabric with a woven pattern (not printed), such as stripes, plaid, or gingham, can help make cutting on the grain easier. Decide how deep you want your fringe to be (ours is 1/4 inch), and mark the distance along the edges of the wrong side of each square with the Clover Chaco Liner. Working on one edge at a time, carefully pull out one lengthwise thread at a time until you get to the chalk line; use a needle to help separate and pull out threads as necessary. After fringing all the edges of both pieces of fabric, lay the two pieces together, wrong side to wrong side, matching up the edges. Pin them together at the center of each side, near the edge, and at the corners, so they stay lined up. Using matching or contrasting thread, sew them together with an even 1/8-inch running stitch about 1/8 inch in from where the fringe starts, removing the pins as you work your way around. Start and stop your stitching between the two layers so all knots are hidden. To use heavier fabric or for a thinner pocket square, use just one layer of fabric, but don't omit the topstitching around the edge, as this helps stop the edges from continuing to fray.

Add a contrast stitch and buttons: Cut out the pocket square, but do not hem yet. With the Clover Chaco Liner and a ruler on the right side of the fabric, mark a line parallel to each edge of the fabric at 1 1/8 inches from the edge, then repeat at 1 1/2 inches in from the edge. Thread a long, slender needle with embroidery floss, top-stitching thread, buttonhole twist, or another thick decorative thread, and tie a knot on the end. Along each chalk line, make a line of even 1/4-inch running stitches from side to side on the fabric. When you begin the line of stitching, make sure to start sewing on the wrong side of the fabric so that the knotted end is on the wrong side and 1/8 inch from the cut edge of the fabric. Don't pull the thread too tight as you sew or the fabric will pucker. When you get to the other edge of the fabric, tie off on the wrong side 1/8 inch from the cut edge and cut the thread. Do this along each chalk-marked line. Hem as usual; the knotted ends of each top-stitched line should be rolled inside the hem so no knots show. Choose your favorite corner, and sew on three decorative buttons.

VARIATIONS

Pocket squares, and the embellishments shown here, can be adapted to any type of fabric, from rustic to elegant. Simply choose fabrics in your palette, or in an appropriate accent color.

FELT BUD BOUTONNIERES

These charming boutonnieres feature a tight, structured flower bud shape that adds a soft touch to groomsmen's attire. They can also be adapted to ladies' corsages by making the flowers slightly bigger. To add dimension, choose three shades in the same palette for the flowers. Felt is forgiving but thick, so be sure to use fabric shears—they'll ensure clean, tidy cuts.

LEVEL

Easy

CATEGORY

Attire

TIME

1 to 2 hours per boutonniere

WHEN TO START

3 to 4 weeks before the wedding

GROUP OR INDIVIDUAL

Individual, or a small group

BUDGET

Less than $50

MATERIALS

Makes 4 boutonnieres

- Three 12-×-12-inch sheets colored wool felt, in varying shades
- One 12-×-12-inch sheet green wool felt
- Thread to match colors of the felt
- Twelve 3 1/2-inch lengths sturdy floral wire, approximately 1/8 inch thick
- 4 corsage pins

TOOLS

- Rotary cutter
- Ruler
- Chalk pencil
- Fabric shears
- Cutting mat or a magazine
- Dressmaker's pins
- Sewing needle
- Leaf templates (available online at www.chroniclebooks.com/handmade-weddings)

HOW TO

1. Fringe the felt.

Using a rotary cutter and ruler, cut a 2-×-5-inch rectangle out of one of the pieces of colored felt. Fold the piece of felt in half lengthwise. Using chalk pencil and the ruler, mark a chalk line parallel to the bottom edge of your felt (not the folded side), 1/4 inch in from the edge (*figure 1, page 43*). Starting 1/8 inch from one end of the felt, use fabric shears to make a series of deep, 1/8-inch-wide cuts into the folded edge of the felt, stopping each cut at the chalk line (*figure 2, page 43*). Repeat until the entire length of the folded felt is fringed.

2. Make the bud.

Lay the folded and fringed felt on your work surface. Shift the top layer of the felt to the right by 1/4 inch, so that the loops cascade at an angle (*figure 3*). Beginning at the right-hand edge with the felt firmly on your work surface, roll the felt tightly from right to left (*figure 4*). Once the felt is completely rolled, check the fringed top to see that you have created the desired effect. The fringed loops should cascade at an angle, creating tight, elegant buds. If the flowers are loose and floppy, unroll and try again, shifting the top layer in the opposite direction before rolling. Place two pins through the rolled edge, forming an X, to hold the roll in place while you sew it together in the next step. Repeat for two more flowers per boutonniere.

3. Attach the bud to the stem.

Using a needle and matching thread, sew the roll tightly into place, keeping an eye on the top of the flower to ensure that it doesn't get distorted. To the extent possible, sew the bottom of the roll closed to create a tapered effect. Insert a 3 1/2-inch piece of floral wire into the center of the base of the flower (*figure 5*). Repeat for each flower.

4. Cover the stem.

Cut a 1/2 × 3-inch length of green felt. Trim to match the length of floral wire that protrudes from one of the felt flowers. Fold the felt in half lengthwise, cutting the end at a 45-degree angle to create a stem shape (*figure 6, page 44*). Using a needle and green thread, use a whip stitch (a stitch that goes over the edge of the fabric) to close the open end of the folded felt: At the base of the folded felt stem, bring your needle through both layers of felt, from back to front. Loop the thread around the open edge of the felt, and bring another stitch through from back to front. Repeat until the entire length of the stem is sewn shut (*figure 6, page 44*). Work the stem onto the floral wire that protrudes from the flower, and add

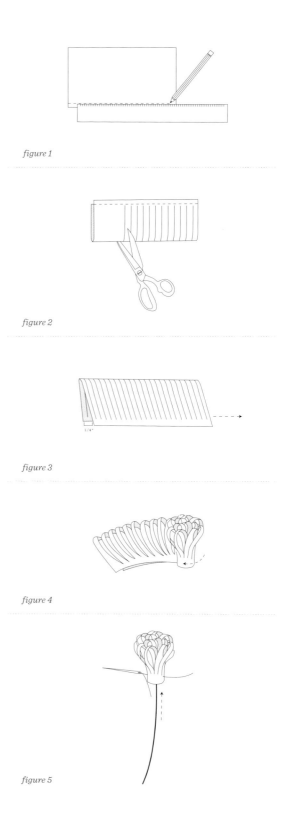

figure 1

figure 2

figure 3

figure 4

figure 5

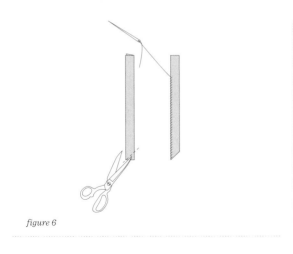

figure 6

figure 7

a few stitches to secure the stem to the flower. Repeat for each flower. Arrange the finished flowers into a nice grouping and secure them together with a few stitches.

5. Attach the leaves.

Using the Leaf template as a guide, cut out two pairs of leaf shapes per boutonniere. Lay the smaller leaf on top of the larger leaf in each pair, and stitch into place. Make a small M-shaped fold or tuck at the base, and stitch it in place about ¼ inch up from the bottom edge, to give the leaf pair a three-dimensional look. Stitch two pairs of leaves to each stem grouping *(figure 7)*.

6. Attach the corsage pin.

Insert a corsage pin into the stem of one of the flowers on each boutonniere. On your wedding day, use this pin to affix the boutonniere into groomsmen's lapels.

VARIATIONS

• **Happy Graphic:** Choose bright reds, yellows, or blues for your flower buds. Instead of shifting the top layer of felt to the right after you have created the fringe, simply fold in half lengthwise and roll. This will result in a flower that has loose, loopy petals.

• **Organic Minimal:** Choose shades of charcoal, ivory, or brown felt for your flowers and stems.

• **Modern Classic:** Choose blacks, creams, and soft accent colors for the flowers, and cut thinner fringed loops for a more delicate effect. If desired, reduce to one or two flowers per boutonniere for a more tailored look.

FELT-FLOWER RING PILLOW

LEVEL
Moderate

CATEGORY
Ceremony

TIME
4 to 6 hours

WHEN TO START
Anytime

GROUP OR INDIVIDUAL
Individual

BUDGET
$50 to $75

This linen ring pillow is decorated with a scattering of simple felt flowers and leaves. To make the flowers feel more organic, we used felt in three different shades (if you are also making the Felt Bud Boutonnieres, page 41, you can use the same three shades). To tie the rings to the pillow, we used seam tape, an inexpensive, delicate ribbon that is available in a range of colors at craft shops or online.

MATERIALS

Makes 1 ring pillow
For the flowers and leaves:
- 4 pieces felt—three shades of the same color for the flowers, and green for the leaves
- Matching threads

For the ring pillow:
- 1/4 yard medium-weight cotton or linen for the inner fabric (this will not show)
- 1/4 yard medium-weight cotton, linen, wool, silk, etc. for the outer fabric (this will show)
- 1 bag fiberfill
- Thread to match the outer fabric
- 1 yard 1/4-inch seam tape or ribbon

TOOLS

For the flowers and leaves:
- Flower Petal and Leaf templates (available online at www.chroniclebooks.com/handmade-weddings)
- Fabric pencil
- Fabric shears
- Sewing needle

For the ring pillow:
- Rotary cutter
- Quilting ruler (we recommend OmniGrid)
- Sewing machine or sewing needle
- Scissors
- Point turner (optional)
- Iron and ironing board
- Straight pins

HOW TO

1. Make the flowers.

The flowers consist of four petal shapes gathered at the base into an M-shaped pleat and sewn together. Using a fabric pencil, trace the flower

petal templates on your felt and cut out with fabric shears, remembering to make four petals per finished flower. Thread your needle with coordinating thread and tie a knot. Make an M-shaped pleat in the narrow base of a petal. Pierce the needle through the folds, then wrap the thread around the folds and pierce the needle back through the folds, cinching tight (*figure 1*). Repeat twice to secure the pleat. Without cutting your thread, pleat your next petal and pierce the needle through the folds, stringing them onto the same thread. Holding the pleated ends together with ends aligned, repeat the cinching stitch. Add the remaining two petals, aligning the ends to form a symmetrical flower shape (*figure 2*). When all four petals are cinched, pull the thread tight, tie a knot, and cut the thread. Repeat to make the remaining flowers.

2. Make the leaves.

Trace the Leaf template onto your green felt and cut out with fabric shears. Repeat the M-shaped pleat technique from step 1, this time tying a knot and cutting the thread once a single leaf is pleated and cinched (*figure 3*). Repeat to make the remaining leaves.

3. Make the pillow insert.

It's important to make a pillow insert to ensure that the lumps in the fiberfill don't show through the fabric of your finished product.

Using your rotary cutter, cut two squares of inner fabric measuring $8\,^3/_8 \times 8\,^3/_8$ inches. This will result in an insert that is $7\,^7/_8 \times 7\,^7/_8$ inches, for an 8-×-8-inch ring pillow ($^1/_2$ inch is used for a seam allowance). If you would like your ring pillow to be a different size, use the following formula: canvas insert = finished size + $^3/_8$ inch. Ring pillow = finished size + $^1/_2$ inch.

Layer the two squares, one on top of the other, wrong-side out. Using a sewing machine or stitching by hand, sew along the edge, $^1/_4$ inch in

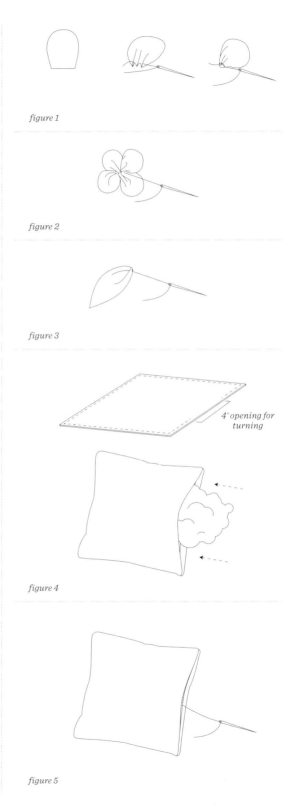

figure 1

figure 2

figure 3

4" opening for turning

figure 4

figure 5

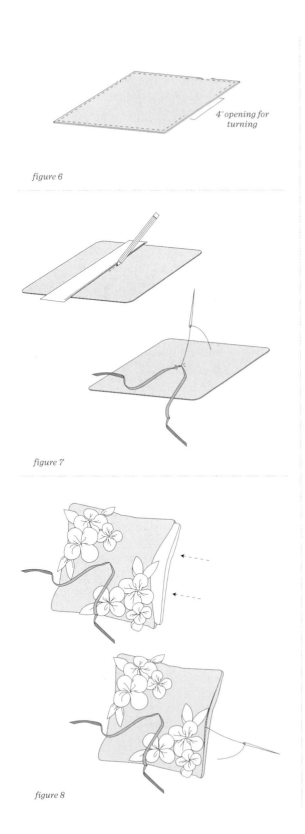

figure 6

figure 7

figure 8

from the sides, using a running stitch (see page 35), to form a C shape, sewing all along the edge except for a 4-inch section at the middle of the fourth side (*figure 4, page 47*). Tie a knot and cut the thread. Turn right-side out, carefully turning the points with a point turner (optional). For a tailored look, iron the seams flat, using the point turner to help iron the corners and any hard-to-reach places; for a softer look (as shown here), don't iron. Gather a handful of fiberfill. Pull apart to smooth out any lumps. Gently stuff it into the pillow insert (*figure 4, page 47*). Sew the open 4-inch section closed using a slip stitch: thread your needle and tie a knot; then bring the needle up through the underside of one folded edge so that the knot is hidden. For each stitch, slip the needle through the fold of the opposite edge for about 1/4 inch; then bring the needle back up and draw the thread through (*figure 5, page 47*). Continue to slip the needle and thread through the opposing folded edges.

4. Make the ring pillowcase.

Using your rotary cutter, cut two squares of outer fabric measuring $8^1/2 \times 8^1/2$ inches. Layer the two squares, one on top of the other, wrong-side out. Sew along the edge, 1/4 inch in from the sides, using a running stitch, to form a C shape. Prior to sewing the third side, turn your fabric right-side out and slip it over the pillow insert. Check to make sure that the insert fits snugly into the ring pillowcase and is neither too loose nor too tight. Mark the placement of the third seam with a pin, remembering that the raw edges of the seam will take up a bit of space, turn inside out, and finish sewing the third side and the rest of the C shape on the fourth side (*figure 6*). Tie a knot and cut the thread. Turn right-side out, carefully turning the points with the point turner (optional). Iron the seams flat, using the point turner to help iron the corners and any hard-to-reach places.

5. Attach the ribbon, flowers, and leaves.

Lay your empty pillowcase on a flat surface. Using a ruler and fabric pencil, mark the center of the square, front and back (*figure 7*). Mark the halfway point of the ribbon and sew it to the front mark at this point (use the back mark to add a tuft in the next step if desired). Trim the loose ends to your desired length, 9 to 10 inches (you can also trim them later, after tying on your rings).

Arrange the flowers and leaves until you are happy with their placement. Pin them into place, being careful not to catch the back of the pillowcase. With your left hand inside the pillowcase to make sure you don't catch the back, carefully sew the flowers and leaves onto the pillow top using a running stitch.

6. Finish the pillow.

Slip your decorated pillowcase over your insert. Sew the open side shut using a ladder stitch: tie a knot in your thread and bring the needle up through one end of the open side. Make a stitch across to the opposite side of the open seam, push the needle down through the seam edge to join the two sides together and, staying on the same side, bring your needle back up about 1/4 inch further along the seam. Repeat, making another stitch back across the opposite edge (*figure 8*). To add a tuft to the center of your ring pillow, thread a needle and tie a small, neat knot. Bring it through the mark on the back of your ring pillow, through to the center of the ribbon on the front of the pillow. Make a small stitch back through to the back; pull gently to tighten slightly; tie a small, neat knot; and cut any excess thread (*figure 9*).

figure 9

VARIATIONS

• **Girly Romantic:** Make the flowers in shades of pale pink, and consider using layers of pretty fabrics instead of felt. Instead of using the same fabric for the top and bottom of the ring pillow, use a neutral linen for the top and a pretty pattern or subtle stripe for the bottom.

• **Organic Minimal:** Make the flowers and leaves in shades of charcoal gray or white.

• **Modern Classic:** In lieu of adding flowers, follow the instructions for making the basic ring pillow. Use tailored striped or solid fabrics to jazz it up, or stitch in a monogram.

VINTAGE-PLATE
TABLE NUMBERS

LEVEL
Easy

CATEGORY
Reception

TIME
20 to 30 minutes
per sign

WHEN TO START
2 to 3 weeks before
the wedding

**GROUP OR
INDIVIDUAL**
Group (after printing)

- *Station 1: Position and cut the
  numbers to the correct shape.*
- *Station 2: Affix the paper to the
  plates.*
- *Station 3: Spray paint the stands.*

BUDGET
$50 to $100

Vintage (or new) plates and serving platters, propped up in a simple painted plate stand, make the perfect vehicle for displaying table numbers. For a group of one hundred guests, you'll only need ten to twelve plates, each available for $5 to $10 on eBay, Etsy, or at flea markets. The plates make great displays for menus and welcome signs, too.

MATERIALS
Makes 10 table-number signs
- 1 can white spray paint
- 10 wooden plate stands
- 10 sheets card stock in ecru,
  white, or a coordinating color
- 10 plates or platters

TOOLS
- Newspaper or a cardboard box
- Table Number templates
  (optional, available online at
  www.chroniclebooks.com/
  handmade-weddings)
- Font: Nelly Script
- Laser or inkjet printer, or a
  felt-tip marker or paint pen
- Tracing paper
- Pencil
- Scissors
- Double-sided tape or glue dots
- Newsprint or bubble wrap,
  for storing

HOW TO
1. Spray paint the plate stands.
Lay newspaper down in a well-ventilated area, or use a medium-sized cardboard box to create a makeshift spray booth. Spray paint the plate stands. Leave to dry for 15 to 20 minutes.

2. Print and cut out the table numbers.
Customize your numbers using one of the online templates, or find a font that you like and type out your table numbers on a computer. Print onto the card stock. Or, write the numbers by hand using a

felt-tip marker or paint pen. Center your tracing paper over the desired plate. Mark the outline of the indented center area using a pencil. Lay the tracing paper over your card stock, aligning to center the number, and tape down. Cut through both layers neatly using scissors, trimming as necessary to fit. Reuse the tracing paper for plates that are the same size.

3. **Adhere the numbers to the plates.**

Using double-sided tape or glue dots, adhere the numbers to the plates. Wrap each plate in newsprint or bubble wrap and store until needed.

VARIATIONS

Although vintage plates would give this project an old-fashioned feel, modern china patterns or bold patterns and solids from the 1950s or '60s can be just as compelling.

- **Happy Graphic:** Use different colors of Fiesta Ware. Or, choose modern white plates in a circle or square shape, and print the table numbers using vibrantly patterned paper. Or, forgo a traditional number, and instead give each table a different color or pattern.

- **Organic Minimal:** Choose handmade plates by local ceramicists or designers with a minimal aesthetic, such as Heath Ceramics.

- **Modern Classic:** Choose classic china patterns from makers such as Royal Copenhagen, Lenox, or Villeroy & Boch. Get more bang for your buck by choosing the pattern for which you're also registered.

FABRIC-WRAPPED FAVORS

LEVEL
Easy

. . . .

CATEGORY
Favors and gifts

. . . .

TIME
10 to 20 minutes per favor

. . . .

WHEN TO START
2 to 3 weeks before
the wedding

. . . .

**GROUP OR
INDIVIDUAL**
Group

. . .

- *Station 1: Cut the fabric.*
- *Station 2: Fill the favor boxes.*
- *Station 3: Wrap the favors.*

. . . .

BUDGET
$150 to $250 for 100
wraps, excluding contents,
depending on fabric cost

These favors use a simple Japanese fabric-wrapping technique known as *furoshiki*. Use it to wrap boxes of candy, chocolate, cookies, or other small gifts. Be sure to pick the contents first, before cutting the material, as the fabric should be neither too tight nor too loose to create an attractive shape.

MATERIALS

Makes 100 favors
- 17 yards lightweight fabric, such as cotton or silk (adjust to match favor size and fabric width)
- Favor box (available from packaging or baking supply stores; optional)
- Favor contents

TOOLS

- 12-inch or longer ruler (we recommend a clear, gridded quilting ruler, such as Omnigrid)
- Large cutting mat (at least 12 × 18 inches recommended)
- Rotary cutter with extra blades

HOW TO

1. Measure your favor and fabric.

Determine the best fabric size given the size of your favor. For a square box, the diagonal line from corner to corner of the square fabric should be a little more than three times the width of the box. This may require some trial and error depending on the shape and size of your favor. The fabric piece should always be square, regardless of the shape of the contents. Using a ruler, mat, and rotary cutter, measure and cut your fabric to the desired size.

2. Wrap the favor.

Square favor: Spread the cloth out in a diamond shape and lay your favor in the center *(figure 1, page 55)*. Tie the ends to your right and left together in a snug square knot. Cross left over right and pull tight into a half knot. Cross right over left and tie another half knot.

Adjust the center to form a flattened squarish shape. Rotate the cloth and tie a second square knot, adjusting the corners to ensure they are neatly tucked in *(figure 2)*.

Rectangular or odd-shaped favor: Spread the cloth out in a diamond shape, and lay your favor in the center. Fold the top end over the favor and tuck it neatly beneath the favor *(figure 3, page 56)*. Fold the bottom end over the favor and leave the corner loose *(figure 4, page 56)*. Fold the right corner toward the center, tucking any excess fabric in as you go. Repeat on the left side. Bring the two ends together and tie in a snug square knot *(figure 5, page 56)*.

3. **If desired, tuck seating or place cards under the knot.**

VARIATIONS

This project can be adapted to just about any style by choosing different types of fabrics. Consider using ready-made scarves as a starting point instead of buying fabric—if you're planning a Western-themed wedding, for example, bandanas in assorted colors are perfect!

- **Girly Romantic:** Consider using vintage lace, chiffon, or organza. Or purchase pretty sari fabric or floral-patterned sheets.

- **Happy Graphic:** Use an assortment of bold patterns by designers such as Alexander Henry, Marimekko, or Thomas Paul (or visit IKEA and turn patterned curtains or sheets into wraps).

(continued on next page)

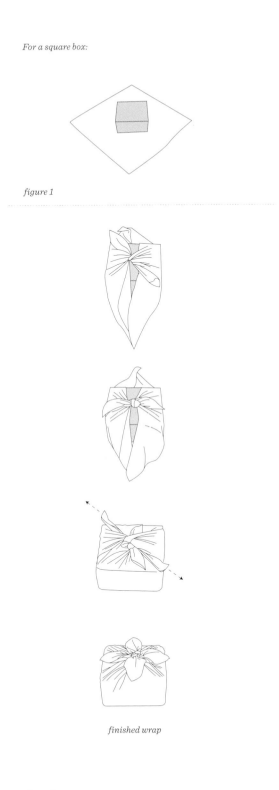

For a square box:

figure 1

finished wrap

figure 2

- **Modern Classic:** Use classic silk or cotton scarves in lieu of purchased fabric—these double as favors in and of themselves.

- **Organic Minimal:** The Japanese roots of this project make it perfect for an organic minimal style. Use muslin, keeping the edges frayed; Japanese cotton fabrics; or lightweight linen in neutral colors and patterns.

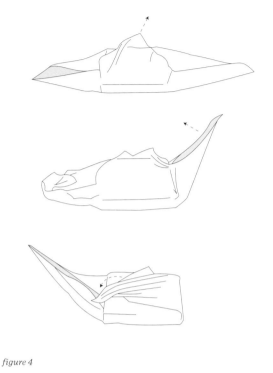

For a rectangular box:

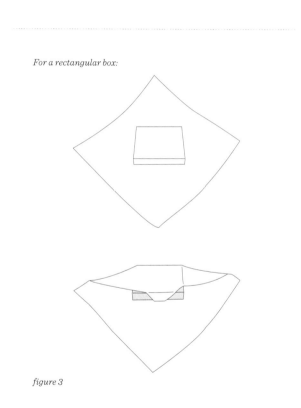

figure 3

figure 4

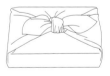

finished wrap

figure 5

NOTES

GIRLY ROMANTIC

ETHEREAL, PRETTY, AND DELICATE, girly romantic style captures the fairy-tale
quality of an ideal wedding. Whimsical, decadent details exist alongside muted colors
and soft textures, creating a dreamlike ambience.

GIRLY ROMANTIC STYLE

PALETTES

Pale pink   Pale lavender   Sea foam   Gold   Cream   Fuchsia (just a hint of)

INSPIRATION

Tim Walker, Marie Antoinette, pastries, Kay Nielsen, Hans Christian Andersen, Jane Austen, *Alice's Adventures in Wonderland*, *A Midsummer Night's Dream*, Victorian paper cuts, Anthropologie catalogs, Agent Provocateur, French General, Maybelle, Michele Papineau, Bernard Maisner, and other fine calligraphers

FONTS

Archive Roman Script, Compendium, Nelly Script, Chanson d'Amour, Dear Sarah Pro, Mrs. Eaves Roman and Small Caps, Engravers' Gothic, Copperplate Light, Copperplate T Medium, SerlioLTStd

TEXTURES

Organza, chiffon, silk, moiré, ruffles, rhinestones, lace, silhouettes, toile

VENUES

Historic hotel or estate, castle, garden, country house, beach, vineyard, field, or farm

DETAILS

Rent etched or gilded glasses or goblets, and look for more ornate (yet tasteful) china patterns for dinner service ✳ *Hang chandeliers over your dining tables, or use tall candelabras* ✳ Have your invitations and seating cards hand calligraphed in gold, black, or brown ink ✳ *Buy a vintage wedding dress* ✳ Create a Mad Hatter's tea service with dessert, featuring mix-and-match teacups, a variety of teapots filled with flavored teas ✳ *Include Pastiglie Leone vintage Italian confections in guest favor or welcome bags* ✳ Look for cosmetics with pretty packaging, such as lip balms, as gifts for your brides-maids ✳ *Serve sweets or cocktails from glass apothecary jars* ✳ Incorporate feathers into your flower arrangements or bouquets ✳ *Wrap your bouquet in vintage velvet ribbon*

PUTTING IT ALL TOGETHER

1.

PALE, PRETTY FLOWERS
Choose romantic flowers in pale, subtle shades: tea roses, ranunculus, and dahlias in very pale pink and peaches; peonies; lisianthus; and lily of the valley.

2.

VINTAGE SILVER
Use vintage trophy cups, champagne buckets, goblets, and bowls for your floral arrangements.

4.

PRETTY COSTUME JEWELRY
Vintage rhinestones and costume jewelry are great on their own, or they can make striking accents for headbands, shoes (attach clip-on earrings to the toes of your shoes), and more.

3.

MACAROONS AND MERINGUES
Serve macaroons, meringues, and other tasty treats alongside coffee. Or offer a dessert bar full of delicious and eye-catching treats in lieu of (or in addition to!) a wedding cake.

Your Presence is Key

Please save the date
to celebrate the marriage of

Lila and Patrick

May 9, 2011
Asheville, North Carolina

Invitation to follow

VINTAGE KEY SAVE-THE-DATE

LEVEL
Easy

CATEGORY
Invitations

TIME
Printing—4 hours
Assembly—4 hours

WHEN TO START
7 to 8 months before
the wedding

**GROUP OR
INDIVIDUAL**
Group (after printing)

· · ·

· *Station 1: Round the corners.*
· *Station 2: Punch the holes.*
· *Station 3: Attach the keys.*
· *Station 4: Address the envelopes.*
· *Station 5: Stuff and seal the
  envelopes.*

BUDGET
$200
(excluding postage)

Inspired by calligrapher and graphic designer Maybelle, this charming save-the-date uses vintage keys to entice your guests. Seam binding, a lightweight and inexpensive ribbon available in a range of colors, gives the card a feminine flare. Look for 3-inch or smaller vintage keys at flea markets, Etsy, or on eBay; the small size will both fit the card and save you money on postage. Note that due to their bulk, these save-the-dates will require extra postage and a hand-cancel fee.

MATERIALS
Makes 100 save-the-dates
- Sixty 8 1/2-×-11-inch sheets card stock
- 100 vintage or reproduction keys, 3 inches or smaller
- 35 yards 1/4-inch seam binding

TOOLS
- Key Save-the-Date template (available online at www .chroniclebooks.com/ handmade-weddings)
- Font: Nelly Script
- Inkjet printer, with extra ink cartridges
- Craft knife
- Ruler
- Cutting mat
- Corner rounder (optional)
- Pencil
- 1/8-inch hole punch, or an awl
- Scissors

HOW TO
1. Make your cards.
Customize your text using the online template and print 60 copies on an inkjet printer (each sheet will yield four cards). Using a craft knife, ruler, and cutting mat, trim the cards to size following the crop marks provided.

2. Embellish your cards.

If desired, round the corners of the cards. Determine the ideal placement of your key on the left side of the card; if you are using a variety of keys, this may vary from key to key. Using a pencil, lightly mark the top center of your key. Using a hole punch or an awl, punch two holes on either side of your mark, about 1/4 inch apart. Cut a 1-foot length of seam binding, and thread back-to-front through your holes. Slip your key over the right end of the ribbon, and tie securely in a bow. Trim the ends of the ribbon at a 45-degree angle.

Note: Because of the weight, rigidity, and variety of the keys, have each save-the-date weighed at the post office before purchasing and affixing postage.

VARIATIONS

The sentiment of this card works well for almost any type of wedding. Alter the look and feel by changing the typeface, envelope color, and ribbon.

- **Retro Homespun:** Tie the key with gingham or stitched ribbon. If desired, back the card with patterned paper or fabric.

- **Happy Graphic:** Use bold, modern fonts and a bright solid ribbon or yarn to tie your key.

- **Modern Classic:** Use wide, black satin ribbons to tie your keys, and tie in a square knot. If desired, edge the card or envelopes using a black or silver paint pen (see facing page).

EMBOSSED & EDGED INVITATIONS

This invitation incorporates embossed details and a gold-edged envelope to create a French patisserie feel. For the embossed portions of the invitation, you must first get a custom rubber stamp made; custom stamps are inexpensive and can be ordered from local stamp makers or online (see "Resources," page 249).

LEVEL
Moderate

CATEGORY
Invitations

TIME
Printing—4 hours
Assembly—6 to 8 hours

WHEN TO START
12 weeks before
the wedding (Invitations
should be mailed 8 weeks
before the wedding.)

**GROUP OR
INDIVIDUAL**
Group (after printing)

- *Station 1: Trim the cards.*
- *Station 2: Rubber stamp the cards.*
- *Station 3: Emboss the cards.*
- *Station 4: Edge the envelopes.*
- *Station 5: Affix postage to the
  envelopes.*
- *Station 6: Stuff and seal the
  envelopes.*

BUDGET
$250
(excluding postage)

MATERIALS

Makes 100 invitations

- Custom rubber stamps
- Sixty 8 1/2-×-11-inch sheets
  ecru or white card stock for
  invitations
- Thirty 8 1/2-×-11-inch sheets
  ecru or white card stock for
  RSVP cards
- Gold stamp pad
- 3 to 4 containers gold embossing powder
- One hundred twenty-five
  A7 envelopes
- One hundred twenty-five
  4-bar envelopes
- Gold paint pen (we recommend Sakura Pen-Touch
  Paint Marker)
- Postage stamps for RSVP card
  and invitation envelopes

TOOLS

- Embossed Invitation
  templates (available online
  at www.chroniclebooks.com/
  handmade-weddings)
- Fonts: Serlio LTStd and
  Nelly Script
- Inkjet printer, with extra ink
  cartridges
- Craft knife, with extra blades
- Ruler
- Cutting mat
- Paper cutter (optional)
- Scrap paper
- Two 8 1/2-×-11-inch sheets
  of cardboard
- Pencil
- Masking tape
- Stapler (optional)
- File folder
- Heat embossing tool
- Glue sticks

*Note: If you are assembling invitations with a group, be sure to have
enough craft knives, rulers, cutting mats, glue sticks, and paint pens
to keep everyone busy—we recommend four of each.*

HOW TO

1. Order your custom rubber stamps.

Customize your monogram and return address using the online templates, and send them to a local stamp maker or online vendor to be made into rubber stamps. A rubber stamp can be made from either a hard-copy printout of your artwork or a high-resolution computer graphics file. Remember that the artwork needs to be the mirror image of what you want to stamp, so be sure to tell the stamp maker what direction you want it to face.

2. Print your invitations.

Customize your invitation and RSVP card text using the online templates and print 60 copies of the invitation on an inkjet printer; each copy will yield 2 invitations. Print 30 copies of the RSVP card; each copy will yield 4 cards.

3. Cut out your invitations.

Using a craft knife, ruler, and cutting mat or a paper cutter, cut the invitations and RSVPs along the crop marks provided. If using a craft knife, as soon as your blade begins to dull, put in a fresh blade.

4. Stamp your invitations.

Press your monogram stamp onto your stamp pad, covering it with a thin, even coat of ink. Make a test print on your scrap paper, and adjust the ink as necessary. To ensure that you stamp in the same place every time, make a cardboard jig. Press your stamp down onto your invitation, and mark the left and top edges lightly with a pencil (*figure 1*). Cut out four 7-×-3-inch strips of cardboard. Align the first two strips so that they form a right angle, and affix masking tape to the front and back of the seam to secure it. Repeat for the second two strips. Push the lower left-hand corner of your invitation into one of the right angles you have just created (*figure 2*). Lay the second right angle on top of the first, shifting up and to the right until the interior edges align with your pencil marks.

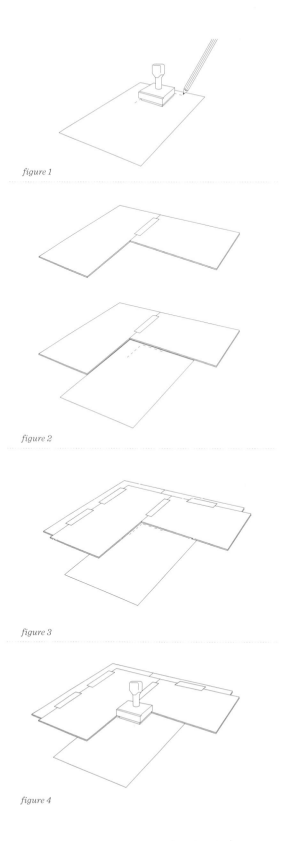

figure 1

figure 2

figure 3

figure 4

Tape or staple the second right angle to the first (*figure 3, page 67*). When you stamp the rest of your invitations, slot the invitation into your jig so that it fits into the first right angle, and then align your rubber stamp to the second right angle (*figure 4, page 67*).

5. Emboss your invitations.

Lay your open file folder on your work surface. Once your invitations are dry, lay them one by one on the file folder and sprinkle the stamped areas with gold embossing powder. Remove the invitations from the folder and pour back the excess powder. Heat the powder on the invitation with a heat embossing tool per the manufacturer's instructions. Repeat for all invitations.

6. Edge your invitation envelopes.

Place an A7 envelope, flap open with glue side down, on your work surface. Lay a second open envelope on top of it, and adjust the placement until 1/8 inch of the first envelope flap is revealed on all sides of the flap. Holding the two envelopes firmly in place with one hand, flip the envelopes over. Using a pencil, mark the bottom edge of the envelope that is now on top onto the envelope below it. Using a ruler and craft knife, cut a straight line where you have marked. The bottom will be your template.

Place an A7 envelope, flap open and facing you with glue side down, on your work surface. Align the bottom edge of your template to the bottom edge of your envelope. Holding the pointed part of the template down, fill in the exposed edge of your envelope flap with your gold paint pen. When you are done, remove the template and touch up any uneven spots with your paint pen, as needed. Edge the rest of the envelopes.

7. Stamp your envelopes.

Press your return address stamp onto your stamp pad, covering it with a thin, even layer of ink. Make a test print on your scrap paper, and adjust the ink as necessary. Stamp the flaps of your A7 envelopes, and the face of your 4-bar envelopes, centering the stamp each time.

8. Assemble the invitations.

Affix postage, collate your inserts, and insert each set into an envelope so that when it is pulled out with your right hand, the invitation is facing the right way up. Seal the envelopes with a glue stick. Address your envelopes, and assemble your invitations (see the appendix "How to Address and Assemble Your Invitations," page 256).

VARIATIONS

Heat embossing is a useful technique and can be used for all types of invitations. Embossing powder is available in a wide range of colors, including both matte and metallic.

- **Organic Minimal:** Emboss loose organic shapes onto your invitations in a pale color, such as sea foam or sage green.

- **Modern Classic:** Using the Modern Classic Invitation template (available online at www.chroniclebooks.com/handmade-weddings) or your own design, emboss a monogram on your invitations.

DYED COFFEE-FILTER POM-POMS

Dyed pale pink, these ethereal coffee filter pom-poms resemble cabbage roses, and they have a dramatic impact when hung in strands radiating from the center of your reception hall or tent. Because of the dyeing and drying time, start this project early, working in batches—especially if you anticipate needing a large number of strands (it can take thirty to forty strands to fill a forty-foot tent).

LEVEL
Easy

CATEGORY
Décor

TIME
12 to 16 hours, plus drying time per group of 6 strands

WHEN TO START
4 to 6 months before the wedding

GROUP OR INDIVIDUAL
Once the filters are dyed, this is a good group project. Have each member make a few pom-pom strands.

BUDGET
Less than $25

MATERIALS
Makes six 20-ft. strands
- 1,000-count box 12-cup wide-base commercial coffee filters, approximately 9 3/4 inches wide
- 1 jar powdered fabric dye (we used Jacquard Acid Dye in "Hot Fuchsia")
- 120-foot length kitchen string

TOOLS
- Clothesline or length of rope
- Drop cloth (optional)
- Large stockpot
- Rubber gloves
- Large mixing bowl or bucket
- Straight pins
- Scissors
- Ruler
- Yarn needle
- Glue gun and glue sticks

HOW TO

1. **Set up your clothesline.**
   Tie up your clothesline in a kitchen or bathroom, or outdoors. The clothesline will be used to dry the dyed coffee filters. Because they are absorbent, the filters will not drip much, but you may wish to cover surfaces around the clothesline with a drop cloth.

2. **Dye half of the coffee filters** (the remaining half will be left white). Fill your pot with water and add the powdered dye according to the manufacturer's instructions. Mix the initial dye batch fairly weakly and add additional dye powder as you go along to get a variety of shades of pink. Weak dye mix will result in a pale pink. The stronger the dye mix, the brighter the pink. The dye will collect at the edges of the filters as they dry to create a darker fuchsia edge. With rubber

gloves on, take a stack of coffee filters. Holding the stack in one hand, pull off individual coffee filters and place them in the dye, submerging them completely. Once you have worked your way through the entire stack, pull out several at a time and squeeze to remove excess dye.

Set the filters in your mixing bowl and repeat until all the dyed filters have been transferred to the mixing bowl. Continue to dye filters and transfer them to the mixing bowl until your bowl is full. Take a ball of dyed coffee filters and pull off an individual filter. Undo any folds and clumping, grasp the filter from the middle of the base, and pin to the clothesline using straight pins. Continue to pin up the rest of the dyed filters. You can pin them close together to get as many filters on your line as possible. Allow them to air-dry completely, overnight.

3. Prepare the coffee filters.

Fold approximately two thirds of your coffee filters into quarters. Flatten the remaining ones. Include a mix of dyed and undyed filters in each group.

4. Assemble the pom-pom strands.

Cut a 20-foot length of string. Thread one end through your yarn needle.

Keeping the filter folded, push the needle through the tapered point of a folded coffee filter. Repeat with 2 to 3 more folded filters *(figure 1)*. Push the filters down the string until they are about 2 feet from the end of the string. With a glue gun, dab a generous bead of glue to the string where the first coffee filter was pierced *(figure 1)*. This will act as a stopper to hold it in place. Continue to thread the needle through coffee filters. Use a mix of darker pink, lighter pink, and undyed filters to create an organic, cabbage rose effect (use more filters for a fuller look). Each pom-pom should consist of 13 to 16 filters in the following order:
- Glue bead
- 3 to 4 folded coffee filters
- 2 flat coffee filters
- 3 to 4 folded coffee filters
- 2 flat coffee filters
- 3 to 4 folded coffee filters
- Glue bead

Once you have threaded all your pom-pom layers, push them together tightly and fix with a bead of glue where the last filter was pierced *(figure 2)*. Continue to make pom-poms along the length of the string, leaving 10 inches or more between pom-poms. The last pom-pom should be about 2 feet from the end of the string.

figure 1

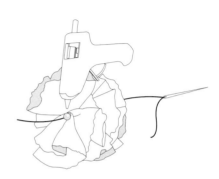

figure 2

VARIATIONS

- **Retro Homespun:** Rather than using coffee filters, use patterned cupcake liners. Assemble per the instructions on page 27.

- **Happy Graphic:** Dye the filters in alternating shades of bright red, yellow, or blue. Use a generous amount of dye to achieve a more saturated color.

- **Organic Minimal:** Dye the filters in strong tea, or use brown or gray fabric dye to create an organic, natural effect.

- **Modern Classic:** Soak the filters in water (no dye necessary) to soften the shape of the filter. Assemble them to create ruffly white pom-pom strands.

FABRIC-FLOWER VEIL

4

These fabric flowers make pretty accents for a headband or veil but can also be used to make hair clips, combs, or corsages. Choose sheer, sturdy fabrics such as organza, chiffon, and lightweight cotton for the best effect.

LEVEL
Moderate

CATEGORY
Attire

TIME
6 hours

WHEN TO START
1 to 2 months before
the wedding

GROUP OR INDIVIDUAL
Individual; however, if you're planning to use these to create hair clips or corsages for bridesmaids, invite them over to make their own!

BUDGET
Less than $25

MATERIALS
Makes 1 veil

- 1/2 yard organza, chiffon, or other lightweight fabric for the fabric flower
- 1/2 yard opaque, lightweight fabric to cover the headband (we used thin cotton—pima, broadcloth, sateen, or batiste also would work)
- 1/2 yard interlining (cotton flannel or medium-weight linen)
- 1 yard seam tape to match your fabric
- 1 yard Russian veiling (a type of netting with wide diamond-shaped openings), at least 18 inches wide (we mixed regular veiling with chenille-dotted veiling)
- Thread to match your fabric, or invisible thread
- 1 buckram bridal headband foundation, measuring 1 1/2 × 10 to 12 inches, available from fabric stores that sell bridal and veiling supplies

Or, to make your own headband foundation:

- Kraft paper, or a brown paper bag (optional)
- 1/4 yard buckram (available at Judith M. Hat & Millinery Supplies, at www.judithm.com, and other fabric stores)
- 1 yard 19- to 20-gauge millinery wire, or thick floral wire

TOOLS
- Fabric Flower templates (available online at www. chroniclebooks.com/ handmade-weddings)
- Quilting ruler (we recommend Omnigrid)
- Cutting mat
- Rotary cutter
- Iron and ironing board
- Straight pins
- Fabric shears
- Fabric pencil (optional)
- Long, narrow sewing needle, such as a darner or millinery needle
- Pencil and eraser (optional)
- Paper scissors (optional)

HOW TO

Step 1: Make the flowers.

1. Cut and iron the fabric.

Cut the flower fabric into three 6-×-28-inch sections using a ruler, cutting mat, and rotary cutter. Fold in half lengthwise, and iron along the fold.

2. Cut out the petal shapes.

Accordion-fold the folded fabric crosswise into equal 4-inch sections. Pin into place *(figure 1)*. Using the Fabric Flower templates provided as a guide, cut out the petal shapes using the folded edge as the base. If desired, trace the template onto the fabric with a fabric pencil before cutting. Unpin the fabric and unfold the accordions, leaving the fabric folded lengthwise. Tidy up any misshapen petals with the fabric shears *(figure 2)*. Repeat for each piece of folded fabric.

3. Sew the flowers.

Thread your needle and tie a knot. Keeping the fabric folded in half lengthwise, start at one end and sew a running stitch (see page 35) along the folded edge. Every 2 inches or so, push the fabric toward the knot so that it gathers at the base. If necessary, secure the fabric in place with a knot before continuing your running stitch. Once the entire length of the flower is sewn and gathered, tie a knot. Sew a couple more stitches through the base of the fabric to hold it in place *(figure 3)*.

Option: You can also layer the flowers, as we have done, with rosettes like on page 179, made of veiling or other fabrics (or both). If using sheer fabrics, secure the rosette ring at the base, but do not sew the cut edges of the ribbon together; the seam will show too much.

Step 2: Make the headband.

1. Make a headband foundation (skip this step if you are using a store-bought foundation). Cut the kraft paper or a brown paper bag into a strip

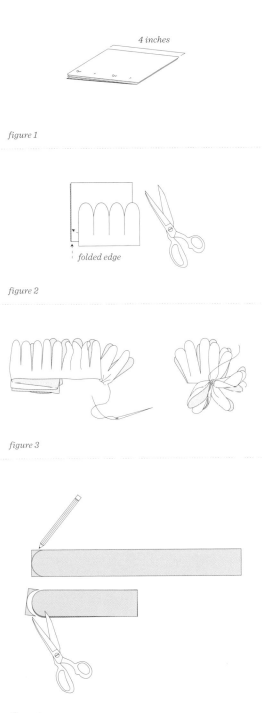

4 inches

figure 1

folded edge

figure 2

figure 3

figure 4

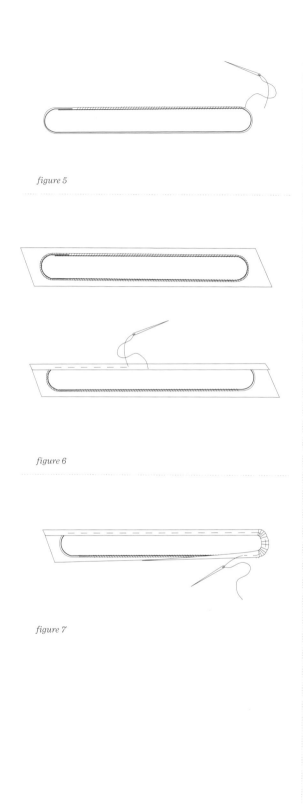

figure 5

figure 6

figure 7

1¹/₂ × 12 inches. With a pencil, on one end of the rectangle, draw a rounded corner, no more than ¹/₂ inch in from the end of the paper. When you get a shape you like, fold the strip in half and cut out both ends along your drawn line so they're symmetrical *(figure 4, page 75)*. Try it on in the mirror to make sure you like the shape and length; make any necessary adjustments. Use this finished paper piece as a pattern to draw the shape onto the buckram, and cut it out. Cut a 1-yard piece of wire, and gently flatten it with your hands so it's not quite as curved as when it was in a roll. Lay one end of the wire against the cut edge of the buckram, on a straight side (not on a curved section). Starting ¹/₂ to 1 inch from the end of the wire, whip stitch the wire to the edge of the buckram, all the way around (see page 43 for whip stitch instructions). Gently bend the wire around the corners as you go. When you get back around to the beginning of the wire, cut the end of the wire off so that it overlaps itself by ¹/₂ to 1 inch. Whip stitch the ends together and to the buckram, securing them in place *(figure 5)*. This side will be the "back" (placed away from the face). Looking in the mirror, gently bend the finished foundation to fit your head, until you get a shape you like.

2. Interline the headband.

You'll want to cover the headband foundation with an interlining, so that the wire does not show through the outer fabric; this will give it more depth and a nicer shape. Using the width and length of the foundation as a guide, cut out a bias strip that is 1 inch wider and longer than the foundation (see page 180 for instructions on cutting bias strips). Lay the bias strip down, and lay the foundation on top of it, inside facing up, and centered. Starting on one lengthwise (straight) edge, fold the fabric up and over the edge of the frame, and stitch through both to secure the cut edge of the fabric to the inside of the frame *(figure 6)*. Work your way around the foundation, securing the interlining as you go, stretching it gently to

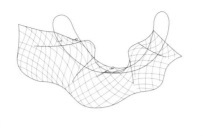

figure 8

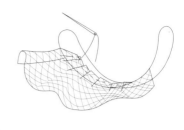

figure 9

smooth any wrinkles. When you get to the curved ends, fold the fabric into small tucks to round the corners, pulling the fabric toward the center of the inside of the headband to remove any wrinkles that form. You may need to carefully cut away excess fabric at the curved ends to get it to lay flat, but be sure to leave enough for it to wrap around to the inside *(figure 7)*.

3. Cover the headband with the outer fabric.

Follow the preceding instructions for interlining, using your outer fabric, except that the bias strip should be 1¹/₂ inches wider and longer than the foundation, so that more of the inside surface of the headband is covered.

4. Create the veil.

Cut a rectangular piece of veiling ¹/₂ yard long and 7 inches wide—you'll notice that one or both long edges of the veiling has a thicker or decorative thread; use this as one long edge of your rectangle. Now, leaving the side with the thicker edge intact, cut the other two corners off diagonally, starting about halfway up widthwise.

5. Attach the veil to the headband.

Lay the headband down, inside edge up. Place the cut edge of the veiling (the side with the diagonal cuts) on the front side of the headband (face side, without the wire join). Pin the cut edge of either end of the veiling to the inside of the headband, about ¹/₂ inch in from either end of the headband. Find the rough center (lengthwise) of the long cut edge of the veiling, and pin it to the rough

center of the inside of the headband *(figure 8)*. Now, evenly pleat and pin the veiling to the inside of the headband. The veiling is longer than the headband, so evenly distribute the extra length by making roughly evenly spaced small tucks in the veiling, pinning them in as you go. Stitch the veiling to the inside center of the headband removing pins as you go *(figure 9)*. Be sure to stitch down the tucks securely.

6. Attach the flowers.

Stitch the flowers to the headband.

VARIATIONS

- **Happy Graphic:** Use brightly colored fabric to make flower combs for your bridesmaids, omitting the veiling. Attach 1 or 2 flowers to each comb, either using hot glue or sewing them to the satin portion of the comb.

- **Organic Minimal:** Choose natural-colored fabrics and create a comb, hair clip, corsage or boutonniere for your bridesmaids or groomsmen. Consider applying these flowers to the DIY ring pillow (see page 45).

- **Modern Classic:** Make the flowers out of white or ivory organza, or embellish with feathers or beads.

RUFFLE ROLL PURSE

5

This pretty roll purse makes a great gift and accessory for your brides-maids. Add dimension by using a pretty ribbon and vintage glass button for the closure and by using a complementary fabric for the lining.

| LEVEL |
| Advanced |

CATEGORY
Attire/Favors and gifts

TIME
4 to 6 hours

WHEN TO START
3 to 4 months before
the wedding

**GROUP OR
INDIVIDUAL**
Individual

BUDGET
$50 to $75

MATERIALS

Makes 1 purse
- ¹/₂ yard outer fabric (medium weight)
- ¹/₃ yard heavyweight iron-on interfacing
- ¹/₃ yard crinoline
- ¹/₂ yard lining fabric
- Matching thread
- 4-inch piece ribbon
- 1-inch button

TOOLS

- Ruffle Roll Purse templates (available online at www. chroniclebooks.com/ handmade-weddings)
- Rotary cutter
- Quilting ruler (we recommend Omnigrid)
- Cutting mat
- Iron and ironing board
- Sewing machine
- Straight pins
- Needle

HOW TO

1. Cut and interface the fabric for the purse.

Using the top and bottom patterns, cut a top and a bottom rectangle from your outer fabric, your interfacing, and your crinoline using a rotary cutter, ruler, and cutting mat. You should end up with six rectangles, two in each fabric.

Place the outer fabric rectangles right-side down on your work surface. Center the corresponding interfacing, right-side up, glue-side down, on each rectangle of outer fabric. Flip the fabric and interfacing so that the fabric is right-side up. Iron per the manufacturer's instructions for interfacing *(figure 1, page 80)*.

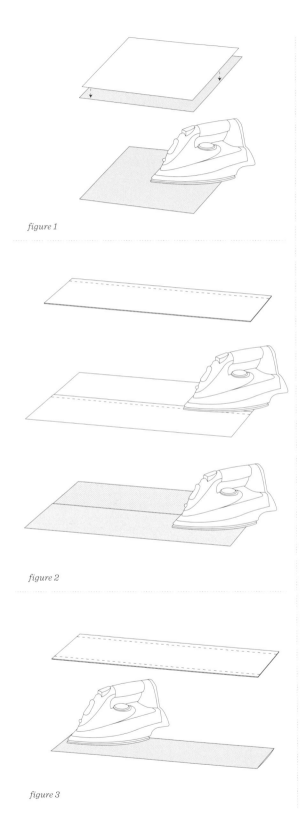

figure 1

figure 2

figure 3

2. Make the box pleats.

Use 1/2-inch seam allowances throughout unless otherwise specified. Using the rotary cutter, ruler, and cutting mat, cut three 2-inch-wide and 45-inch-long strips of both the outer fabric and lining fabric to make the box pleats. The fabric should be folded selvedge (self-finished edge) to selvedge and cut along the grain.

Align a set of strips, right-sides together, on your work surface. Sew along one edge with a 1/4-inch seam allowance. Iron the seam allowance open, fold along the seam with the fabric right-side out, and iron again (figure 2). Repeat for the second strip set.

For the third set, place the strips right-sides together and sew along both sides, creating a tube. Turn right-side out and press (figure 3).

Fold each strip into a box pleat: Fold the fabric toward you, then fold it away, so that the resulting fold is 1/4 inch wide and is shaped like an S. Pin the pleat in place, with the pin running parallel to the short edge of the strip (figure 4). Skip about 1/2 inch of strip, and fold it away from you to meet the fold you just made. Then fold back in the opposite direction; this time the fold will be shaped like a Z. Pin into place. Skip 1/2 inch of strip and repeat, butting each fold up against the next. Continue until the pleated strip measures at least 15 inches. Using a sewing machine, sew the pleats into place on the first two strips. Sew along the raw edge using a running stitch and matching thread, about 1/8 inch from the edge. Remove the pins as you go (figure 5).

Leave the third strip pinned, not stitched (this will be the top row of pleats). Because you'll want all of the box pleats in alignment when sewing them to the purse top, we recommend pleating the entire length of each strip set and using the sections that look best.

3. Stitch the box pleats to the purse.

Stitch the box pleats to the front of the purse, starting with the bottom row—the bottom edge of the pleats should align with the first set of notches. Continue in the same manner for the second row of pleats overlapping the first row by about ¹/₈ inch *(figure 6)*.

For the third set, make sure that the box pleat row is securely pinned down. The stitches will be visible on this row so stitch slowly.

4. Stitch the ribbon loop.

Place the ribbon loop so that the edges are on either side of the notch on the top pattern piece that specifies ribbon placement *(figure 7)*. Stitch into place.

5. Sew the outside of the purse.

Lay the front and back pieces of the purse on your work surface, right-sides down, and center a piece of crinoline over each piece. Stitch the crinolines into place with a basting stitch (this is a big stitch just to hold things in place, meant to be cut out later) *(figure 8, page 82)*.

Place the front and back pieces of the purse on your work surface, right-sides together. Using a running stitch (see page 35), stitch along the two short sides and the long side with a ¹/₂-inch seam allowance *(figure 9, page 82)*.

Iron the seam allowance open so that it lays flat. Snip off the bottom corners about ¹/₈ inch from the sewn edge to reduce bulk *(figure 10, page 82)*. Cut out the basting stitches and remove the thread. Turn the purse right-side out.

6. Make the lining.

Cut out your purse lining pieces, following the template. Place them back-to-back, wrong-sides out, on your work surface. Using a running stitch, sew along the two short sides and one long side

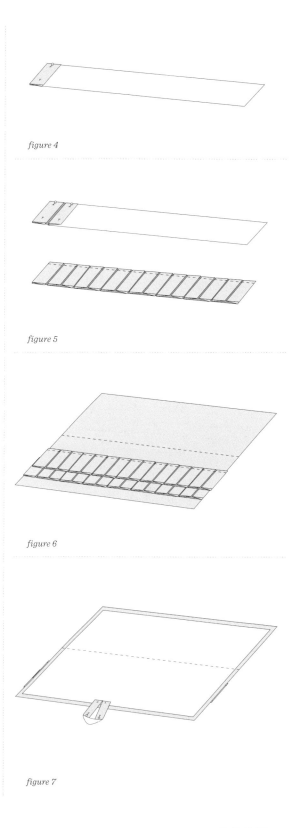

figure 4

figure 5

figure 6

figure 7

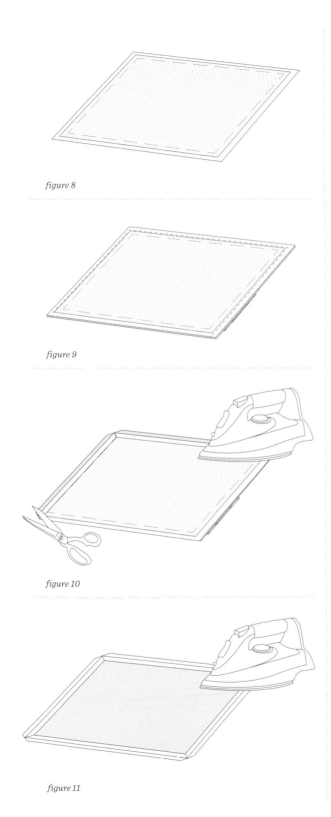

figure 8

figure 9

figure 10

figure 11

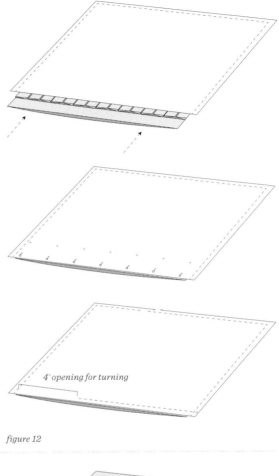

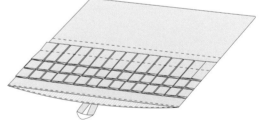

4" opening for turning

figure 12

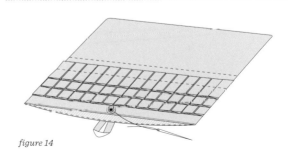

figure 13

figure 14

using a $1/2$-inch seam allowance. Iron the seam allowance open so that it lays flat. Snip off the bottom corners about $1/8$ inch from the sewn edge to reduce bulk. Leave inside out *(figure 11)*.

7. Sew the lining into the purse.

Turn the lining inside out. Place the outside of the purse, right-side out, inside the lining. The two right sides will be facing each other. Match the side seams and pin around the top raw edge. Stitch around the top of the purse using a $1/2$-inch seam allowance. Leave a 4-inch section open for turning *(figure 12)*. Pull the lining through the opening so both pieces are now right-side out and the raw edge is hidden *(figure 13)*. Now, push the lining into the outside of the purse. Pin the opening closed using a slip stitch about $1/4$ inch from the edge (for instructions, see page 48).

8. Iron the purse and add the button.

Iron the purse flat, then fold it in half, and iron again for a crisp fold. Sew the button, centered right below the first row of box pleats *(figure 14)*.

VARIATIONS

- **Organic Minimal:** Make the purse out of linen, and fray the edges of the ruffles.

- **Modern Classic:** Make the purse using solid black, white, or pale pink fabric with a striped or dotted liner.

TEACUP CENTERPIECES

6

LEVEL
Easy

CATEGORY
Reception

TIME
2 to 3 hours

WHEN TO START
Prepare the teacups and floral foam 4 to 6 weeks before the wedding

•

Arrange the flowers the morning of or the day before and store in a cool place.

GROUP OR INDIVIDUAL
Group
Have each group member make a handful of arrangements, or use stations.

. . .

• *Station 1: Prepare floral foam and soak in water.*
• *Station 2: Trim the stems.*
• *Station 3: Arrange the flowers.*

BUDGET
$150 to $250, depending on teacup cost and types of flowers chosen

Vintage or new teacups and saucers make lovely centerpieces that are also very easy to arrange. Collect a variety of teacups in your palette, and then choose coordinating flowers, keeping the scale of the cups in mind (the flowers should be small enough so that three to four large buds and five to six smaller buds fit in each cup).

MATERIALS
Makes 30 centerpieces
• 30 teacups, with or without saucers
• 6 to 8 bricks Oasis floral foam
• Flowers—3 to 4 large stems and 5 to 6 smaller stems per cup

TOOLS
• Ruler
• Craft knife or butter knife
• Bucket or large bowl
• Sharp knife or scissors

HOW TO
1. Prepare your floral foam.
Measure the rough dimensions of each teacup and use a craft knife or butter knife to cut a corresponding piece of floral foam so that it fits snugly in the cup. It's OK if the brick protrudes slightly over the lip of the cup, since it will eventually be entirely covered in flowers. Insert the foam into the cups.

2. Arrange your flowers.
When ready to use, soak each piece of floral foam in a bucket or large bowl of water. Trim your flower stems to the desired length, cutting at a 45-degree angle with a sharp knife or scissors (using a dull blade will impede water flow and reduce the life of your flowers).

To arrange your flowers, slide the stems into the floral foam. Arrange smaller flowers into clusters of two or three.

SCALLOPED CUPCAKE STAND

7

LEVEL
Moderate

CATEGORY
Reception

TIME
4 to 8 hours

WHEN TO START
4 to 6 weeks before
the wedding

**GROUP OR
INDIVIDUAL**
Group

· · ·

• *Station 1: Cut out the crosspieces.*
• *Station 2: Double paste the pieces.*
• *Station 3: Cut out the trim.*
• *Station 4: Cover the pieces
in paper.*
• *Finish individually: Assemble
the tower and affix the trim.*

BUDGET
$50 to $75

This tiered cupcake stand is a lovely way to display cupcakes, adding flourish to your festivities. Cardboard cake boards provide the basic structure, which are transformed with pretty papers and decorative trim. If you're running short on time, transport the stand flat to your ceremony site. You can also buy an inexpensive prefabricated cardboard stand (from www.cupcaketree.com). However, note that prefabricated trees have many notches; these allow you to assemble and disassemble without glue, but take more time to cover.

MATERIALS

*Makes 1 cupcake stand, holding
approximately 50 cupcakes*

• Three 17-×-24-inch cake boards
(purchase 6 boards if they are
less than 1/4 inch thick)
• Two round cake board in each
of the following diameters:
6-inch, 10-inch, 14-inch, and
18-inch.
• Eight 24-×-36-inch sheets solid
paper for covering bases (we
used sea foam–embossed paper
from Bell'occhio)
• One 24-×-36-inch sheet contrasting paper for scalloped
trim (we used Gold Moiree
from Bell'occhio)

TOOLS

• Scallop template (optional;
(available online at www.
chroniclebooks.com/
handmade-weddings)
• Craft knife, with extra blades
• Ruler
• Cutting mat
• Glue sticks
• 1-inch scallop ruler, or 1 sheet
card stock for Scallop template
• Pencil
• Scissors
• Bone folder
• Hot glue gun
• Pins

*Note: If using a prefabricated cupcake tree, skip steps 1 and 2. For step 6,
assemble the tree per the manufacturer's instructions—typically the pieces
fit together like a puzzle, and no glue is required.*

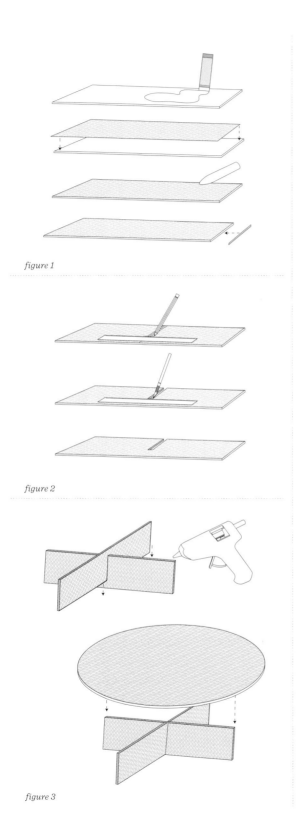

figure 1

figure 2

figure 3

HOW TO

1. Cut out the crosspieces.

Using your rectangular cake boards, a craft knife, ruler, and cutting mat, cut out the following rectangles (if your boards are less than 1/4 inch thick, double the number for each size):

- Two 3 × 4 inch
- Two 3 × 8 inch
- Two 3 × 12 inch
- Two 3 × 16 inch

2. Double paste the round cake boards and the crosspieces.

Using a glue stick, apply glue liberally to one cake board and press firmly to a second board of the same size, being careful to align the edges perfectly. Repeat for each of the cake boards and for each pair of crosspieces (if you cut out four of each). Let everything dry.

3. Cut out your scalloped trim.

Using a craft knife and ruler, mark and cut out eight 1 3/4-×-36-inch strips from your contrasting paper, being careful to maintain a straight edge. Align the straight edge of your scallop ruler along one edge of a strip, and trace the scallops with a pencil. If you do not have a scallop ruler, cut out the Scallop template provided, and trace it onto card stock. Cut it out with scissors, and use it as your template. Cut out the scalloped trim with scissors. *Note: In lieu of a scalloped border, feel free to use any decorative edge punch.*

4. Cover the cake boards and crosspieces.

Trace two outlines of each round cake board onto your paper—one to cover the top and one to cover the bottom. Cut them out carefully using scissors. Using a glue stick, apply glue to the top of each round, and lay the corresponding paper on top, making sure to align the edges. Smooth with the bone folder. Repeat for the bottom side of each round. Use a craft knife to trim off any excess.

Using a craft knife, ruler, and cutting mat, cut out paper strips to cover the crosspieces:

- Four 3 × 4 inch
- Four 3 × 8 inch
- Four 3 × 12 inch
- Four 3 × 16 inch
- 16 strips 3 × 1/4 inch, or the width of the crosspieces

Using a glue stick, apply glue to one side of each crosspiece, and lay a corresponding strip over it *(figure 1),* making sure to align the edges. Smooth with your bone folder. Repeat for the second side. Smooth with your bone folder. Let dry. Affix the 1/4-inch strips to the ends of each crosspiece to create a crisp edge.

5. Cut notches out of the crosspieces.

Mark out a 1/4-inch-wide × 2-inch-deep slot in each crosspiece: Using a pencil, draw a line down the middle of each rectangle. Draw a line 1/8 inch to either side of this line. Draw a perpendicular line 2 inches from the upper cardboard edge. Cut out the slots using a craft knife, ruler, and cutting mat *(figure 2).*

6. Assemble the tower.

Slot each pair of crosspieces together to form an X. Starting with the largest cake round, apply hot glue to the top edges of the corresponding X. Center the cake round on top of the X and press down firmly, holding it in place for a few minutes until the glue dries *(figure 3).* Take the next largest X and apply hot glue to the bottom edges. Center it on the largest cake round. For increased stability, align the X so that it is rotated 45 degrees from the previous X. Press down firmly, holding in place until the glue dries. Repeat for all layers of the tower.

7. Attach the trim.

Using a glue stick, apply glue to the trim. Attach a length of trim, aligning the straight edge to the top of the round *(figure 4).* Pin the end of the trim to the edge of the cake round. Pull the trim taut and affix around the edge, adding glue as necessary. Remove the pin when dry, and cover the hole with an overlapping piece of trim. Continue until the edges of all the rounds are decorated with trim.

Tip: If you are planning to transport your cupcake stand flat to your reception site, enlist a bridesmaid to assemble the stand and attach the trim the day before the wedding.

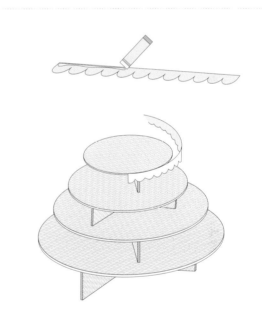

figure 4

VARIATIONS

This cupcake stand can be adapted to any color palette or style simply by adjusting the papers and trims you choose.

• **Retro Homespun:** Cover the boards with pretty solid, floral, stripe, or polka dot paper or fabric. Use decorative cupcake wrappers (available in ginghams, polka dots, and stripes) for your cupcakes.

• **Happy Graphic:** Cover the boards in a bold solid color, such as red, yellow, or blue. Trim with a solid contrasting grosgrain or twill ribbon.

• **Modern Classic:** Cover the boards in a solid black paper or fabric. Trim with striped ribbon.

PICTURE-FRAME CHARM NECKLACES

LEVEL
Easy

CATEGORY
Favors and gifts

TIME
1 hour

WHEN TO START
1 to 2 months before
the wedding

**GROUP OR
INDIVIDUAL**
Individual

BUDGET
Less than $25

These simple charm necklaces make lovely keepsakes for your brides-maids. Start with a picture-frame charm (available at most beading stores), and use pretty patterned fabric or paper or a printed monogram. Diamond Glaze (a clear glasslike sealer) provides permanent protection though it can dull the artworks' appearance.

MATERIALS

Makes 3 necklaces

- 3 picture-frame charms or lockets
- Patterned fabric, patterned paper, or magazine pages
- 3 yards 1/4-inch or 3/8-inch satin ribbon
- Paper gift tag (optional)
- Small gift or jewelry box (optional)

TOOLS

- Tracing paper
- Pencil
- Scissors
- Gem-Tac adhesive or craft glue
- Tweezers
- Diamond Glaze (optional)
- Scrap paper (optional)
- Small paintbrush (optional)

HOW TO

Note: If you are printing your own artwork (e.g., a monogram or clip art) and plan to seal it with Diamond Glaze, use a laser printer. Water-based inks commonly found in inkjet printers will run once the Diamond Glaze is applied.

1. Cut out your artwork.

Place your tracing paper over the frame, and trace the interior area with a pencil. Cut out a rectangle roughly 1/4 inch around the traced shape. Place it over your fabric or paper, aligning it over the area you'd like to feature. Cut out the shape.

2. Affix your artwork.

Dab Gem-Tac or craft glue onto the back of the artwork. Using tweezers, place the artwork into the center of the frame. Allow it to dry completely.

3. Add the Diamond Glaze (optional).

To prevent air bubbles, squeeze some Diamond Glaze onto a piece of scrap paper until it flows out of the tip. Maintaining pressure on the bottle, gently squeeze Diamond Glaze over the artwork until it is completely covered and slightly mounded in the center. Remove any bubbles by dabbing them with a paintbrush. Let dry completely, approximately 30 minutes.

4. Attach the ribbon.

Thread the ribbon through the charm. If necessary, fold the ribbon in half and cut at a 45-degree angle to allow for easier threading. Trim the ends so that the necklace is the desired length. Tie the ends in a knot or bow. If desired, print or handwrite a paper gift tag to your bridesmaids and attach it to the charm, and/or place the charm in a small gift or jewelry box.

VARIATIONS

By adjusting the ribbon color and fabric or artwork, this project can be adapted to a variety of styles and venues. For example, choose clip art of starfish or shells for a beach wedding or horseshoes for a rustic or Western wedding.

- **Retro Homespun:** Use a retro-patterned fabric for your artwork. If desired, embroider it with the bridesmaids' initials.

- **Modern Classic:** Cut out a silhouette of each bridesmaid's profile (trace a photograph on tracing paper, then cut it from black construction paper and glue onto an oval paper backing).

PAPER-WRAPPED FAVORS

Wrapped with a lovely structured fold and sealed with a personalized label, hand-milled soaps make lovely parting or welcome gifts for your guests. Label the soaps with their "flavors" as well as your names and wedding date. This technique is also adaptable to other types of favors, such as chocolates, candies, or teas. Place them in a glassine bag or rectangular favor box, then wrap them in paper.

LEVEL
Moderate

CATEGORY
Favors and gifts

TIME
4 to 6 hours

WHEN TO START
1 to 2 weeks before
the wedding

**GROUP OR
INDIVIDUAL**
Group (after printing)

. . .

• *Station 1: Cut the paper.*
• *Station 2: Punch the labels.*
• *Station 3: Wrap the favors.*

BUDGET
$200,
depending on favor cost

MATERIALS

Makes 100 favors
• Ten 8 1/2-×-11-inch sheets label stock
• Eighteen 19-×-27-inch sheets decorative paper, in two to three patterns
• 100 pieces hand-milled soap, preferably oval in shape

TOOLS

• Favor Label template (available online at www.chroniclebooks .com/handmade-weddings)
• Fonts: Copperplate T Medium and Nelly Script
• Laser or inkjet printer
• Paper cutter, or craft knife, ruler, and cutting mat
• 2-inch oval punch
• Glue dots (optional)

HOW TO

1. Make your labels.

Customize your soap description(s) using the online template. Or create your own label design using a graphic-design or word-processing program. Print onto label stock using a laser or inkjet printer. If using the template, use a paper cutter or craft knife to trim a rectangle around each label, and then punch using an oval punch, holding the punch upside down so that you can align the outline of the oval with your paper. If designing your own label, mark and measure the labels and trim to size.

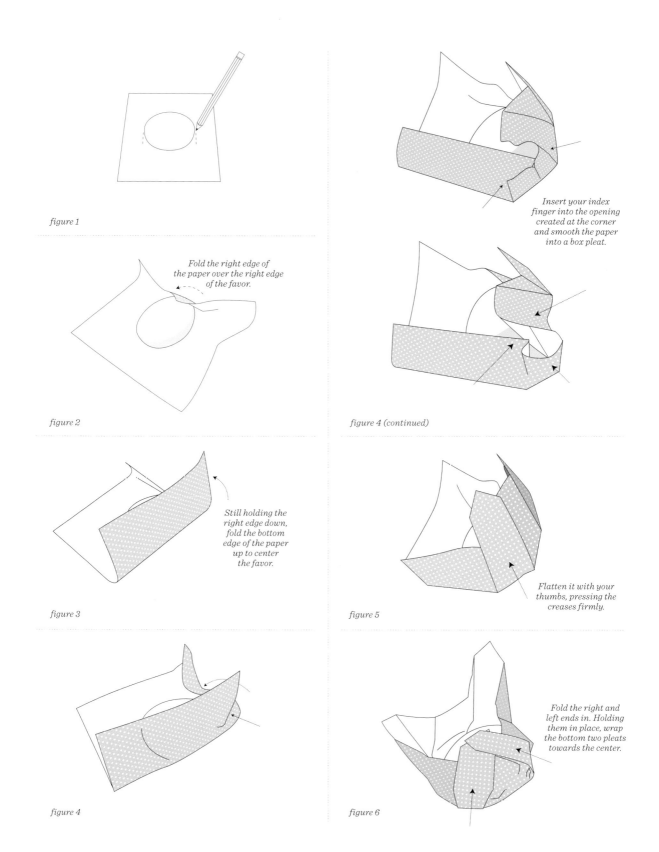

figure 1

Fold the right edge of
the paper over the right edge
of the favor.

figure 2

Still holding the
right edge down,
fold the bottom
edge of the paper
up to center
the favor.

figure 3

figure 4

Insert your index
finger into the opening
created at the corner
and smooth the paper
into a box pleat.

figure 4 (continued)

Flatten it with your
thumbs, pressing the
creases firmly.

figure 5

Fold the right and
left ends in. Holding
them in place, wrap
the bottom two pleats
towards the center.

figure 6

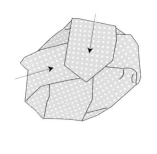

figure 7

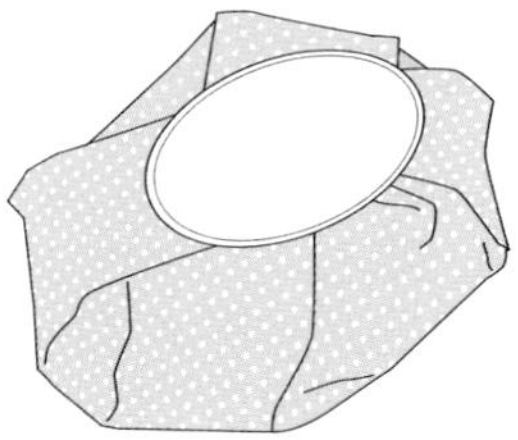

figure 8

2. Wrap your favors.

Determine the best size for your decorative paper. It should be a square with a diagonal that measures three times the length of your favor. Our bar of soap was 3 3/4 inches long, and our paper was 7 × 7 inches (9 3/4 inches along the diagonal). Wrap a test favor first, to confirm the correct size, before cutting all your paper to size.

Lay your cut paper right side down on a flat work surface. Center the soap on the paper, with the long side facing you. Mark the right and left ends of the soap with a pencil *(figure 1)*.

Fold the right edge of the paper over the right end of the soap and hold it in place using the middle finger on your right hand, holding the soap in place with your left hand *(figure 2)*. Still holding the right edge down, fold the bottom edge of the paper up to the center of the soap and hold it down with your left middle finger *(figure 3)*. Insert your index finger into the opening created at the corner, and smooth the paper into a box pleat *(figure 4)*. Flatten it with your thumbs, pressing the creases firmly *(figure 5)*. Repeat with the bottom left corner, holding the bottom edge of the paper firmly in place and allowing the bottom right pleat to loosen as you work on the next pleat.

Rotate the soap on your work surface and work the opposite two corners. When you have completed all your folds, wrap the soap completely. Fold the right and left ends in. Holding them in place, wrap the bottom two pleats towards the center *(figure 6)*. Refold the top two pleats over the bottom two pleats *(figure 7)*. Once you are happy with their appearance, glue a label over the center where the pleats meet *(figure 8)*. If desired, secure the folds with glue dots before attaching the label.

VARIATIONS

- **Retro Homespun:** Wrap your favors in pretty patterned papers. Tie with striped baker's twine.

- **Organic Minimal:** Wrap your favors in thin cotton fabrics or neutral patterned papers.

- **Modern Classic:** Print your monogram on the label, or add a wax seal.

HAPPY GRAPHIC

BOLD, COLORFUL, AND CHIC, a happy graphic wedding is
spirited and fun. Incorporating wit and whimsy, each element inspires
your guests to kick back, relax, and enjoy the celebration!

HAPPY GRAPHIC STYLE

PALETTES

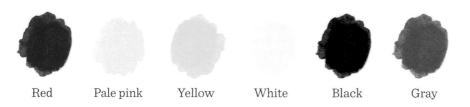

Red Pale pink Yellow White Black Gray

INSPIRATION

Paul Rand/*Sparkle and Spin*, Jonathan Adler, Andy Warhol, Marimekko, Charley Harper, Eric Carle, Charles Eames, and Ray Eames

FONTS

Strangelove Text, Slim Pickens, Register Sans Serif, Oklahoma-Deputy, P.T. Barnum, Futura, Impact, Chalet Paris Nineteen Sixty, American Typewriter, BPreplay

TEXTURES

Graph paper, loose-leaf paper, chipboard, chalkboard, newsprint, newspaper, glossy surfaces, wood grain, collage, primary colors, graphic shapes (hearts, circles, squares, triangles), yarn, scribbles

DETAILS

Rent modern ghost chairs for your reception, and pair them with white linens and colorful napkins ✱ *Use crisp white dishes and simple modern flatware* ✱ Spray paint table-number stands and decorative frames for menus, table numbers, or signage in bright, happy colors ✱ *Create a lounge environment using modern chaises and sofas, with brightly colored accent pillows* ✱ Place jars of colored pencils on each table along with a stack of blank cards. Encourage guests to write a message or draw a portrait of the bride and groom to include in the guest book ✱ *Make your getaway in a colorful Beetle or Mini Cooper* ✱ Make colorful paper flags for cocktails or cupcakes ✱ *Rent a photo booth, or set up a DIY one by hanging a bold fabric backdrop* ✱ Provide chalkboard word bubbles, mustaches on sticks, funny glasses, hats, and brightly colored picture frames as props

1.

CONVERSE SNEAKERS

Classic and colorful, old-school Chucks make a fun, inexpensive addition to your groomsmen's wardrobe, and you can even design your own. Pair with striped socks if desired!

2.

BIG, ROUND BALLOONS

Available from specialty balloon suppliers (look for 17-inch jumbo round Tuf-tex latex balloons), big, round balloons are irresistible for their simplicity and graphic impact. If you're planning to use a lot of them in your décor, purchase balloon clips, which will make tying them off go more quickly. Don't forget pretty string or baker's twine!

PUTTING IT ALL TOGETHER

3.

PARTY BLOWERS

A fun confetti alternative, these create a festive fanfare to celebrate your "I do's." Place them in a basket at the entrance to the ceremony, or hand them out with programs.

5.

SODA POP AND STRIPED STRAWS

Serve an array of tasty and colorful sodas to refresh guests as they arrive for the ceremony. Buy them locally, or check out POP The Soda Shop (www.popsoda.com) for an exhaustive selection. Serve with colorful striped straws, like those available from Kikkerland (www.kikkerlandshop.com).

4.

BRIGHT, BOLD FLOWERS

Bold flowers—like peonies, dahlias, poppies, or African daisies—add pop to your table décor and bouquets.

MORE HAPPY GRAPHIC DETAILS

Take a photo of yourselves holding giant balloons or chalkboard word bubbles with a message (such as "We're getting hitched!"), and use it to create save-the-date cards or thank-you notes ✳ *Transform bold patterns in your palette into striking stamps using PhotoStamps or Zazzle (www.photostamps.com or www.zazzle.com)*

SPARKLE & SPIN
INVITATIONS

LEVEL
Advanced

CATEGORY
Invitations

TIME
10 to 12 hours

WHEN TO START
14 to 18 weeks before
the wedding (Invitations
should be mailed 8 weeks
before the wedding.)

**GROUP OR
INDIVIDUAL**
Individual, however it
can be handy to enlist help
to line the envelopes and
assemble the invitations.

. . .

- *Station 1: Cut out the envelope liners.*
- *Station 2: Affix the envelope liners.*
- *Station 3: Address the invitation envelopes.*
- *Station 4: Affix the postage.*
- *Station 5: Collate the invitations and enclosures.*
- *Station 6: Stuff and seal the envelopes.*

BUDGET
$200 to $500

Inspired by Paul Rand's classic 1950s children's book *Sparkle & Spin*, this whimsical invitation is silk-screened on chipboard to achieve a graphic, handmade look. The most difficult aspect to silk-screening is making the screens (you'll need one for each color per piece you are printing), and it is especially important to have high-quality screens when printing invitations because of the amount of small type. As a result, we recommend sending your art to a local or online screen-printing shop, such as Standard Screen Supply Corporation (www.standardscreen.com) to have your screens made. Alternatively, you can try one of the many emerging DIY screen-making alternatives, such as PhotoEZ from EZ Screen Print or a silk-screening kit (you'll need to purchase extra screens), which are available at most art supply stores. However, be sure to do a test print well in advance of when you need to mail your invitations.

MATERIALS
Makes 100 invitations
- Custom screens (see project introduction)
- Seventy-five 8 1/2-×-11-inch sheets chipboard for invitations
- Forty 8 1/2-×-11-inch sheets chipboard for RSVP cards
- 15 to 20 pieces scrap paper cut to invitation (5-×-7-inch) and RSVP (3 1/2-×-5-inch) sizes for practice runs
- Water-based screen-printing ink in white, red, and black
- Twenty 8 1/2-×-11-inch sheets label stock, such as Strathmore Writing Label
- One hundred to one hundred twenty-five A7 envelopes
- One hundred 4-bar envelopes
- Postage stamps for invitation and RSVP envelopes

TOOLS
- Sparkle & Spin Invitation templates (available online at www.chroniclebooks.com/ handmade-weddings)
- Font: Strangelove Text
- Inkjet printer, with extra cartridges
- Craft knife, with extra blades
- Cork-backed metal ruler
- Cutting mat
- Newsprint
- Set of 2 hinge clamps (see "Resources," page 249)

(continued on next page)

- A wood board at least 1/2 inch thick and several inches wider and longer than the silk-screen frame
- Screwdriver
- Four 1/2-inch-long screws
- Sharpie
- 2-inch-wide masking tape
- A small prop, such as an art eraser
- Spoon
- Squeegee
- Bone folder
- Envelope moistener with adhesive (optional)

HOW TO

1. Customize your artwork and make your screens.

Customize your invitation and RSVP card using the online templates. Note that each silk-screened ink color is printed in a separate pass, so you will have a total of seven files: three for the invitations (white, red, and black), and four for the RSVP cards (two per side, white and black). To save time and money, the RSVP labels are inkjet-printed. Send your files to a screen printer to have screens made, or make them with a home screen-making kit, following the manufacturer's instructions.

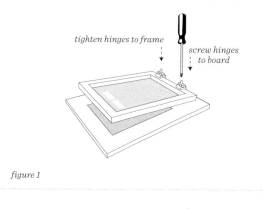

tighten hinges to frame
screw hinges to board

figure 1

figure 2

2. Trim your chipboard.

Using a craft knife, ruler, and cutting mat, cut one hundred fifty 5-×-7-inch chipboard cards for your invitations, and one hundred fifty 3 1/2-×-5-inch cards for your RSVPs. The extra cards are for inevitable mistakes as you are printing each screen. To cut the chipboard, make a series of shallow cuts (do not try to cut all the way through in one pass as this will dull the blade more quickly). As soon as your blade begins to dull, put in a fresh blade.

3. Prepare your silk-screening station.

Cover a 2-×-3-foot work area with newsprint. Attach both hinge clamps to one of the shorter edges of your largest screen frame. The clamps should be close to the corners of the frame, and the frame should be screen-side down and as far into the clamps as it can go. Tighten the clamps enough so they will not shift on the frame.

Lay the frame on the wood board, screen-side down. The frame and hinge clamps should all be entirely on the board. Line up the edges of the hinge clamps' screw plates with one edge of the board so as to leave as much extra board space around the screen frame as possible. Using a screwdriver, attach the four 1/2-inch screws to the hinge clamps to secure the board tightly to the frame (*figure 1*).

Using a Sharpie, trace the outline of the screen frame onto the board *(figure 2)*. You do not need to trace the side that is attached to the hinge clamps. This traced outline will be a guide to help you position the next frame in the exact same place.

If there are any areas of your screen that you don't want to print, but that are not blocked or covered with emulsion, cover them with masking tape.

4. Position your test paper.

Place a sheet of scrap paper on your board, lowering the screen over it and adjusting its position until the artwork is correctly aligned on the paper. Lift the screen into the up position and mark the bottom left and top right corners of your paper on your board with masking tape. These will be your registration marks—they will ensure that your paper is placed in the same location for each print *(figure 3)*.

5. Make a test print and print the first color.

With the frame propped up and in the down position, squeeze or spoon a line of the printing ink (approximately 1 tablespoon) along the top edge of the screen *(figure 4)*. Remove the prop, then take your squeegee and drag the ink from the top edge toward you, across the design area, applying pressure as you pull *(figure 5)*. Carefully raise the frame to the up position and view the print. Insert a new piece of test paper, making any adjustments to the placement of the paper (moving your registration tape accordingly) and amount of ink. Using your spoon, scrape excess ink from the squeegee back onto the top area of the screen, adding ink if necessary. Make additional test prints until you are happy with the quality and placement of the print. Build up the masking-tape marks with chipboard scraps so that the paper won't shift when you are printing *(figure 6)*. Print the first color onto chipboard. Let the cards dry completely before printing the next color.

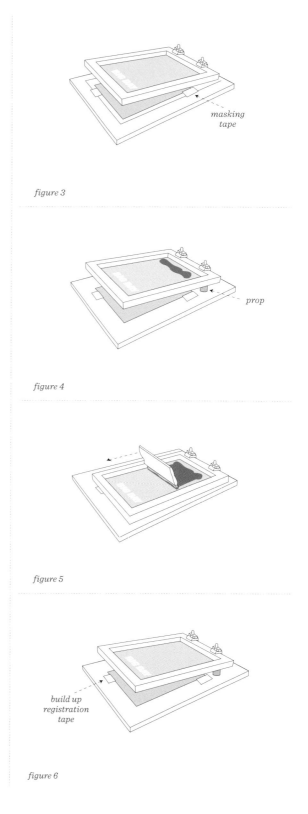

figure 3

figure 4

figure 5

figure 6

6. Print the RSVP cards.

Repeat steps 3, 4, and 5 for all four screens.

7. Make the RSVP labels.

Customize the RSVP address labels using the online template. Print 15 copies onto label stock using an inkjet printer (each sheet yields eight labels). Trim along the crop marks using a craft knife, ruler, and cutting mat.

8. Collate and assemble your invitations.

Affix the RSVP labels to the 4-bar envelopes, centering them and leaving a $1/4$-inch space from the bottom edge of the envelope for postal bar codes. Address your envelopes, and assemble your invitations (see the appendix "How to Address and Assemble Your Invitations," page 256).

VARIATIONS

Silk-screening is a great technique, once you get the hang of it. Create your own design in a graphics program such as Adobe Illustrator, or cut and paste different graphics and text from different sources, such as a word-processing program, onto paper and make a photocopy of each master. Just remember to lay out each ink color separately.

PAPER-LINK CHAINS

LEVEL
Easy

CATEGORY
Décor

TIME
4 to 6 hours

WHEN TO START
2 to 3 months before
the wedding

**GROUP OR
INDIVIDUAL**
Group

· · ·

• Station 1: Cut the strips.
• Station 2: Double paste the strips.
• Station 3: Assemble the chains.

BUDGET
Less than $50

With their bold colors and graphic patterns, these double-sided paper link chains add punch to your reception décor and are simple to make. Colorful gift wrap makes a good starting point, or you can download and print any of the patterns shown here.

MATERIALS

Makes six 20-foot chains

• Seventy-five 11-×-17-inch sheets text-weight paper, or equivalent, in a mix of patterns or solid colors, or one hundred fifty 8 1/2-×-11-inch sheets blank text-weight paper (if printing the paper pattern templates)

TOOLS

• Paper pattern templates (available online at www .chroniclebooks.com/ handmade-weddings; optional)
• Inkjet printer and extra ink cartridges (optional)
• Paper cutter, or a craft knife, ruler, and cutting mat
• Glue sticks
• Bone folder, or a ruler

HOW TO

1. Make the paper strips.

Cut out seven hundred twenty 1 1/2-×-11-inch strips of paper, approximately 120 strips per chain, or 60 double-sided links per chain (about 4 double-sided links per foot). Decide which two papers you would like to use for each chain. Place them back-to-back on your work surface. Dab with just enough glue to hold in place (this will ensure that the two sides align perfectly). Cut into strips. If you are making a lot of chains, it may be worth paying a local print shop to cut the strips using a professional paper cutter. Apply glue to the wrong side of a strip, align it back-to-back with a contrasting strip, and press firmly. Smooth it with a bone folder or ruler. With the glue still wet, curve the strip in the direction you'll be making the loop and smooth. Let it dry. Repeat for all strips. This can be done in batches if desired.

2. Make the chains.

Apply glue to one end of a double-sided strip, loop it around, and secure it to the opposite end with a 1/2-inch overlap. Thread the next double-sided strip through the loop you've just created, and make a second interlocking loop. Continue until you've made a chain of the desired length, alternating patterns as you go, if desired.

VARIATIONS

- **Retro Homespun:** Use gingham, stripe, or floral patterned papers. Or use fabric treated with a liquid fabric stiffener; the treated fabric will hold its shape. To stiffen large amounts of fabric, lay the fabric in a shallow tray and use a paintbrush to apply the fabric stiffener until the fabric is completely saturated. Let it dry completely. Then, cut the fabric into strips using a rotary cutter, ruler, and cutting mat. Glue the links using a fabric adhesive, such as Fabri-Tac.

- **Modern Classic:** Use tailored patterns, such as stripes, dots, houndstooth, and solids.

- **Found:** Recycled papers such as brown grocery bags, newspaper, and magazines make great materials for chains. Collect these over the months before your wedding and separate by color. To achieve a more polished look, make the chains in a limited palette of colors and textures.

KATHRYN PARKER   MARSHALL DEAN, JR
BRIDESMAIDS   GROOMSMEN
CHLOE MCADAMS   JOEL FULLER
HELEN BROOKS   GEORGE YOUNG
FLOWER GIRL   RING BEARER
ELLA MCADAMS   HENRY MCADAMS

THANK YOU
WE ARE HONORED TO BE SURROUNDED
BY OUR CHERISHED FAMILY & FRIENDS

CEREMONY OF
JASON EDWARD DEAN
8, 2011

PARENTS OF THE GROOM
ROBIN & MARSHALL DEAN

BEST MAN
MARSHALL DEAN, JR

GROOMSMEN
JOEL FULLER
GEORGE YOUNG

RING BEARER
HENRY MCADAMS

YOU
BE SURROUNDED
AMILY & FRIENDS

BP + JD

BP + JD

JD

THE MARRIAGE CEREMONY OF
BRITTANY MARIE PARKER + JASON EDWARD DEAN
AUGUST 18, 2011

PARENTS OF THE BRIDE   PARENTS OF THE GROOM
KRISTINE & FRED PARKER   ROBIN & MARSHALL DEAN

MAID OF HONOR   BEST MAN
KATHRYN PARKER   MARSHALL DEAN, JR

BRIDESMAIDS   GROOMSMEN
CHLOE MCADAMS   JOEL FULLER
HELEN BROOKS   GEORGE YOUNG

FLOWER GIRL   RING BEARER
ELLA MCADAMS   HENRY MCADAMS

THANK YOU
WE ARE HONORED TO BE SURROUNDED
BY OUR CHERISHED FAMILY & FRIENDS

THE MARRIAGE CEREMONY OF
BRITTANY MARIE PARKER + JASON EDWARD DEAN
AUGUST 18, 2011

PARENTS OF THE BRIDE   PARENTS OF THE GROOM
KRISTINE & FRED PARKER   ROBIN & MARSHALL DEAN

MAID OF HONOR   BEST MAN
KATHRYN PARKER   MARSHALL DEAN, JR.

BRIDESMAIDS   GROOMSMEN
CHLOE MCADAMS   JOEL FULLER

HEART-SHAPED PROGRAMS

LEVEL
Easy

CATEGORY
Ceremony

TIME
4 to 6 hours

WHEN TO START
1 to 2 weeks before
the wedding

**GROUP OR
INDIVIDUAL**
Group (after printing)

- *Station 1: Cut out the hearts.*
- *Station 2: Assemble the hearts
  and handles.*

BUDGET
$50 to $75

These adorable programs double as fans for an outdoor summer wedding. Place one on each seat at your ceremony, perhaps with a colorful party blowout in lieu of confetti. Note that this program works best if your ceremony is brief. For longer ceremonies, consider adapting the Patterned-Paper Programs (page 139) by using bold graphic patterns from elsewhere in your wedding.

MATERIALS
Makes 100 programs
- Two hundred twenty
  8 1/2-×-11-inch sheets red
  card stock
- 100 wood fan handles

TOOLS
- Heart-Shaped Program
  template (available online at
  www.chroniclebooks.com/
  handmade-weddings)
- Font: Strangelove Text
- Laser or inkjet printer, with
  extra ink cartridges
- Scissors
- Pencil
- Double-sided tape gun and
  extra tape (we recommend
  the 3M Scotch ATG 700
  Transfer Tape Dispenser),
  or glue sticks

HOW TO
1. Customize and print your programs.
Customize your program text using the online template. Print 110 copies of each side of the program onto red card stock using a laser or inkjet printer (10 copies are for inevitable mistakes when cutting). Using scissors, cut each program into a heart shape, following the outline on the template and being careful to cut inside the line so the outline doesn't show.

2. Assemble your programs.

Place your hearts back-to-back. Try to pair up hearts that match each other as closely as possible, as there will be some inconsistencies due to the hand cutting. Once you are happy with your pairings, take the first two hearts and lay them side-by-side, right-sides down, on your work surface. Center a fan handle on one of the hearts, left to right, and position it vertically so that the top 6 inches of the handle lie inside the heart, and the bottom 3 inches lie outside of it, forming the handle. Mark the handle position on the heart with a pencil. Dispense glue or double-sided tape on one side of the top 6 inches of the handle and press into place (*figure 1*). Dispense glue or double-sided tape along the heart-shaped areas of the same heart as well as the second side of the handle. Align the second heart, right-side up, over the glued side and press down firmly (*figure 2*). Repeat for all programs.

VARIATIONS

Paddle fans, as these types of fans are known, can be made in any shape—a circle, oval, square, rounded square, egg, leaf, or traditional fan shape (resembling a quarter circle). If you have a longer ceremony, you can print on both sides of the fan, adding a bit of decorative flourish along the borders.

- **Organic Minimal:** Use a circle or oval shape. Rubber stamp or stencil a pattern onto one side (for techniques see pages 143 to 144 and 157 to 158).

- **Modern Classic:** Make the fans in a tapered circle or oval shape. Adhere a silhouette of the bride on the fan that will go on the bride's (left) side of the ceremony, and a silhouette of the groom on the groom's (right) side (for techniques see pages 175 to 177). Tie a ribbon at the base of each handle.

figure 1

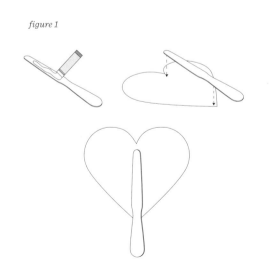

figure 2

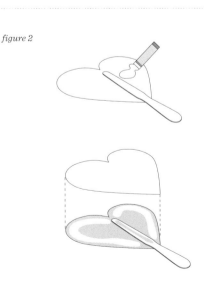

DECAL TABLE NUMBERS

LEVEL
Easy

CATEGORY
Reception

TIME
1 hour

WHEN TO START
1 to 2 weeks before
the wedding

**GROUP OR
INDIVIDUAL**
Group
Have each person affix
numbers to a couple of
bottles, and you're done!

BUDGET
$50 to $75, using store-bought,
rather than rented, bottles

Glass water bottles do double duty as table numbers by applying simple vinyl number transfers. These are available in standard fonts and colors from hardware and art supply stores. Inexpensive custom versions can also be ordered online in almost any font or color. Apply the numbers to glass water bottles, wine bottles, or vintage milk bottles. Or rent glass bottles from your caterer—the numbers will peel off easily and won't cause damage.

MATERIALS

Makes 10 table numbers

- Ten 3-inch vinyl numbers, either Chartpak Vinyl numbers (available from art supply stores) or custom numbers from an online supplier such as www.vinyl-decals.com
- 10 glass bottles, such as the 33 3/4-ounce Giara Bottle from Fishs Eddy; similar bottles are also available at some restaurant supply stores

TOOLS

- Fonts: BPreplay

HOW TO

1. Choose fonts, colors, and table numbers.

Decide on the decal color that best suits your wedding. If using custom decals, search for free online fonts that match your wedding style. We used BPreplay from www.dafont.com. Order as many numbers as needed. Keep in mind that if you are using long tables, you may want a number on either end to make it easier for guests to find their seats. If you are using king's tables (long tables that can seat as many as fifty guests), divide the table into 8- to 10-foot sections, and assign a number to each section.

2. Affix the numbers to the bottles.

Affix the numbers to clean, dry bottles. Avoid any seams in the bottle, and keep the number placement consistent. Ask your caterer to fill the bottles with water, wine, or a colorful punch or cocktail.

VARIATIONS

- **Girly Romantic:** Choose a script font for your numbers, and fill the bottles with pink lemonade or a pale pink cocktail.

- **Organic Minimal:** Use white numbers for a clean, modern look.

SILK-SCREENED PLACE MATS

5

These whimsical kraft paper place mats offer guests a mock place setting and work for both buffet-style or plated service. Place a charger and napkin on the place mat, as shown on the opposite page, or have it double as a place card by writing guests' names in the middle of the plate. If silk-screening feels out of your league, consider just photocopying these in black onto white paper!

LEVEL
Moderate

CATEGORY
Reception

TIME
4 to 6 hours

WHEN TO START
6 to 8 weeks before
the wedding

**GROUP OR
INDIVIDUAL**
Individual

BUDGET
$100 to $150

MATERIALS

Makes 100 place mats

- Custom screen (see page 103)
- One 11-×-17-inch sheet of plain paper (optional)
- One hundred fifty 12-×-18-inch sheets kraft paper, such as Borden & Riley #840 Kraft Pad
- Water-based screen-printing ink in white

TOOLS

- Place Mat template (available online at www.chroniclebooks.com/handmade-weddings)
- Newsprint
- Set of 2 hinge clamps (see "Resources," page 249)
- A wood board at least 1/2 inch thick and several inches wider and longer than the silk-screen frame
- Four 1/2-inch-long screws
- Screwdriver
- A small prop, such as an art eraser
- 2-inch-wide masking tape
- Squeegee
- Spoon
- Chipboard or cardboard scraps

HOW TO

1. Make your screen.

Send the Place Mat template file to a screen printer to have a screen made, or print the template on an 11-×-17-inch sheet of paper and make it with a home screen-making kit, following the manufacturer's instructions.

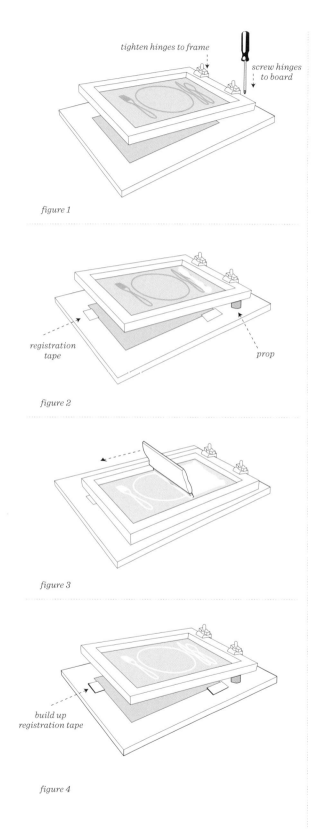

tighten hinges to frame

screw hinges to board

figure 1

registration tape

prop

figure 2

figure 3

build up registration tape

figure 4

2. Prepare your silk-screening station.

Follow the instructions on page 104 for preparing your silk-screening station *(figure 1)*, but do not outline your screen frame with a Sharpie. Follow the instructions on page 105 for positioning your test paper; use a spare sheet from your kraft pad.

3. Make a test print.

With the frame propped up and in the down position, squeeze or spoon a line of the printing ink (approximately 1 tablespoon) along the top edge of the screen *(figure 2)*. Remove the prop, then take your squeegee and drag the ink from the top edge toward you, across the design area, applying pressure as you pull *(figure 3)*. Carefully raise the frame to the up position and view the print. Make any adjustments to the placement of the paper (moving your registration tape accordingly) and amount of ink. Using your spoon, scrape excess ink from the squeegee back onto the top area of the screen, adding ink if necessary. Make additional test prints until you are happy with the quality and placement of the print. Build up the masking-tape marks with chipboard or cardboard scraps so that the paper won't shift when you are printing *(figure 4)*.

4. Print your place mats.

Print the rest of your place mats. Lay them out to dry completely.

VARIATIONS

This simple concept lends itself easily to a number of different wedding styles, such as Organic Minimal or Found, with no changes. To customize, consider using a different ink or paper color or using clip art or your own hand drawing to adapt the place setting to a different style.

• **Girly Romantic:** In lieu of the Place Mat template, download Victorian clip art of a plate and silverware and lay them out in a design program such as Adobe Illustrator.

BRIDE & GROOM CAKE TOPPER

6

With a little creativity, guy and girl wooden doll blanks can be transformed into an adorable personalized cake topper. Simply follow the templates or sketch out your own interpretation (you may want to get a couple of extra doll forms in case of mistakes).

LEVEL
Moderate

CATEGORY
Reception

TIME
4 to 6 hours

WHEN TO START
3 to 4 weeks before
the wedding

**GROUP OR
INDIVIDUAL**
Individual

BUDGET
Less than $25

MATERIALS

Makes 1 cake topper

- 3 1/2-inch-tall male and female wood dolls (available on Etsy or at craft stores)
- Acrylic paints (we used white, red, brown, and black)
- Thread
- 20 to 25 seed beads (we used red)
- Small piece of tulle for the veil
- Decorative button for the veil
- Decorative button or cabochon for the bouquet
- 6-×-1-inch Styrofoam disc (available at craft and floral supply shops)
- One 8 1/2-×-11-inch sheet patterned or solid text-weight paper
- 1 yard 1-inch ribbon

TOOLS

- Pencil
- Paper plate
- Small square brush
- Small pointed brush
- Cup of water
- Paper towel
- Beading needle, or "sharp"
- Scissors
- Hot glue gun and glue sticks
- Ruler
- Pin (optional)

HOW TO

1. Paint the figurines.

Lightly mark your design on the figurines in pencil. Customize the features to match both you and your fiancé– have fun! Squeeze a dab of each paint color onto your paper plate. Wet your brush in your cup

of water, dab on some paint, test the brush stroke on the plate, and begin painting. If the brush is too wet, blot excess water on a paper towel, apply more paint, and try again. Use the square brush for larger solid areas, such as the hair or clothing, and the pointed brush for fine details. Rinse your brush thoroughly in water before switching colors. Let the figurines dry.

2. Add the necklace.

Thread the needle, knotting the thread at one end. String the beads onto the thread until the necklace is long enough to just fit around the bride's neck. Tie the loose ends around the neck in a firm knot and trim with scissors.

3. Add the bouquet and veil.

Cut a 1-×-2-inch piece of tulle (larger for a longer or fuller veil). Accordion-fold it, and attach it to the head with a dab of hot glue. Add a button on top using hot glue. Attach a decorative button or cabochon flower for the bouquet using hot glue.

4. Decorate the base.

Trace the styrofoam disc twice onto your paper, and cut out both circles using scissors. Measure the height of your styrofoam base and cut a strip of solid paper that measures as follows: [height of base] × [circumference of base + 1/2 inch]. *Note: Circumference = diameter × 3.14*. Wrap the paper strip around the side of the base, carefully aligning the top and bottom. Affix with hot glue. Align a circle to the top of the base and affix with hot glue. Repeat for the bottom. Wrap the ribbon around the base, and pin or hot glue in place, aligning its seam with the seam in the paper strip. If desired, add a separate bow to the front of the ribbon.

5. Attach the bride and groom.

Using hot glue, attach the bride and groom to the base. Be sure they are facing away from the seams in the paper and ribbon.

VARIATIONS

- **Retro Homespun:** Cover the base in gingham or striped fabric. If desired, add more features to the figures. Or make your figurines out of wooden clothespins and dress them in tiny fabric outfits. (See www.thesmallobject.com for inspiration!)

- **Found:** Cover the base in found papers, such as kraft paper, tissue paper, recycled gift wrap, or old maps.

KRAFT WELCOME BAGS

7

Kraft five-pound coffee bags make perfect welcome bags for your guests; they're large enough to fit a bottle of soda or water and other necessities and treats. Each one is decorated with a rubber stamp and sealed with a heart-shaped brad. If desired, use the brad to also attach a welcome letter to your guests. Colorful pastry bags can also be used in lieu of kraft bags, and Bulldog clips, either silver or spray painted in different colors, can replace the heart shapes for a more utilitarian look.

LEVEL
Easy

CATEGORY
Favors and gifts

TIME
4 to 6 hours

WHEN TO START
1 to 2 weeks before
the wedding

GROUP OR INDIVIDUAL
Group

· · ·

- *Station 1: Stamp the bags.*
- *Station 2: Punch the holes.*
- *Station 3: Fill the bags.*
- *Station 4: Close the bags with brads.*

BUDGET
$100
(excludes welcome bag contents)

MATERIALS

Makes 100 welcome bags

- Custom rubber stamp (see "Resources," page 249)
- 8 1/2-×-11-inch scrap paper
- Large black stamp pad
- One hundred twenty 6 1/2-×-4 1/2-×-16-inch (5-pound) kraft coffee bags (we got ours from U.S. Box, www.usbox.com)
- Welcome bag contents
- One hundred 1/4-inch-diameter red heart brads (available from Papier Valise, www.papiervalise.com)

TOOLS

- Kraft Welcome Bags template (available online at www.chroniclebooks.com/handmade-weddings)
- Pencil
- Craft knife
- Ruler
- 1/8-inch hole punch

HOW TO

1. **Customize and order your rubber stamp.**

   Customize and send the Kraft Welcome Bags template to a local rubber stamp maker or online vendor to be made into a rubber stamp. Ask them to mount the stamp with no handle, as this will allow you to apply pressure over a large area using the palms of your hands. Or make your own border design by using a computer graphics program or drawing it by hand. A rubber stamp can be made with either a hard-copy printout of your artwork or a high-resolution computer graphics file. Remember that the artwork needs to be the mirror image of what you want to stamp, so be sure to tell the stamp maker what direction you want it to face.

2. **Stamp the kraft bags.**

To ensure consistent placement of the stamp, place the bottom edge of your bag on a piece of scrap paper and mark the bottom two corners of the bag with a pencil. Place your stamp on your work surface face up, and blot the ink pad onto it to ensure even coverage. Press your stamp down onto the bag, and mark the bottom edge of the stamp on your scrap paper with a pencil. Lift the stamp up and check the alignment. Replace the bag, and do another test print, adjusting the stamp and marking the new position until you are happy with the alignment of the print. Carve away any unwanted flecks or spots in your stamp with a craft knife. When you are happy with the print, stamp your kraft bags. Let them dry.

3. **Punch the holes.**

Fold the top of each bag down approximately 1 inch and make a light pencil mark in the middle of the flap, halfway across and halfway down from the fold. Punch a hole at that spot.

4. **Fill and close the bags.**

Fill the bags with favors and amenities for your guests. Some ideas include soda pop, such as Izze's or any of the sodas available at POP The Soda Shop (www.popsoda.com); local cookies or chocolates; a local map or guidebook; hangover cures; slippers; or a favorite book. Fold the flap down, and insert and flatten the brads to close.

VARIATIONS

- **Organic Minimal:** Choose a more minimal font, or replace the text with a patterned band, inspired by the Stenciled Table Runner (page 155) or Rubber-Stamped Confetti Bags (page 143).

- **Retro Homespun:** Instead of a heart brad, fasten with a clothespin. Or use basic white or colored pastry bags. Scallop the top edge using scalloped-edge scissors or a rotary paper cutter with a scalloped blade. Fold the top of the bag over and punch two holes, about 2 inches apart, using a 1/8-inch hole punch. Thread a 10-inch length of 1/4-inch ribbon through the holes, back to front, and tie in a bow at the front of the bag.

- **Modern Classic:** In lieu of coffee bags, use black or white paper handled bags or pastry bags. Print your monogram, silhouettes, or names and wedding date onto a decorative label and attach to the front. Tie a bow to the bag handles.

BUTTON SEATING CARDS & FAVORS

8

Decorative buttons make fun favors, and the patterns or icons double as a fresh take on traditional table numbers, with a different one assigned to each table. Tied to a favor box with string or yarn, they also serve as an eye-catching embellishment. A button-making machine and supplies require a sizable up-front investment, but you can reuse the machine afterward for party favors and more.

LEVEL
Easy

CATEGORY
Favors and gifts

TIME
4 to 6 hours

WHEN TO START
1 to 2 weeks before the wedding

GROUP OR INDIVIDUAL
Group (after printing)

· · ·

- *Station 1: Cut out the circles.*
- *Station 2: Make the buttons.*
- *Station 3: Assemble your favors.*

BUDGET
$300 to $350 (including button-making machine and equipment; excludes favor box contents)

MATERIALS

Makes 100 seating cards and buttons, and ten table numbers

- 6 sheets text-weight paper for patterns
- One hundred 1 1/4-inch button-making parts: shells, Mylar discs, and pin backs (available from Dr. Don's Buttons, www. buttonsonline.com)
- 20 sheets card stock for tags and table numbers (optional)
- One hundred 2-×-2-×-2-inch kraft favor boxes
- Favor box contents (candies, chocolates, novelty items)
- 50 yards thin yarn, ribbon, or twine

TOOLS

- Button Pattern, Seating Tag, and Table Number templates (available online at www. chroniclebooks.com/ handmade-weddings)
- Laser or inkjet printer, with extra cartridges
- Circle cutter (available from Dr. Don's Buttons)
- 1 1/4-inch button-making machine (we recommend the Mini Magic button press from Dr. Don's Buttons)
- Craft knife, with extra blades
- Ruler
- Cutting mat
- Glue stick (optional)
- Scissors

HOW TO

1. Make the buttons.

Using a laser or inkjet printer, print 6 copies of the Button Pattern templates onto text-weight paper; each template yields 20 buttons. Choose your patterns and decide on the number needed of each

julian abdey

hope james

wood

tricia roush

ole

pattern (corresponds to the number of guests at each table). Cut out the button patterns using the circle cutter. Follow the manufacturer's instructions for making your buttons. For the Mini Magic, insert the metal shell (the front part of the button) into the machine, sharp-edge down, followed by a button pattern and a Mylar disc. Rotate the dies. Place the pin back into the machine, sharp-edge up (and pin back facing down). Push the handle down, and pull the handle up. Rotate the dies. Push the button down, and pull the handle up. You will now have a complete button. Repeat for all buttons.

2. Print out the seating tags and the table numbers (optional).

Customize the Seating Tag template with your guests' names. Print onto card stock using a laser or inkjet printer. Alternatively, print out the blank templates and fill in guests' names by hand. Print the Table Number templates onto card stock. Trim the tags and cards along the crop marks provided in the templates using a craft knife, ruler, and cutting mat. As soon as your blade begins to dull, put in a fresh blade. If desired, glue two of each Table Number card back-to-back to make them sturdy; display them in table number stands.

3. Assemble your favor boxes.

Put your favor contents into your kraft boxes. Cut a 30-inch length of yarn, ribbon, or twine. Center your favor, right-side down, on your ribbon. Cross the ribbons over each other, and holding the ribbon tight, flip your box right-side up and pull the ribbon toward the center of the box. Tie a knot and trim the ribbon ends short. Pin your button over the knot and tuck the seating tag under it.

VARIATIONS

- **Retro Homespun:** Use an assortment of vintage-inspired patterns such as florals, ginghams, or stripes. For a winter wedding, consider using tartans or plaids. Note that the patterns should ideally be scanned and printed onto paper. Fabrics are difficult to cut using the circle cutter and tricky to use with a button maker (if you do attempt it, leave out the Mylar disc).

- **Modern Classic:** Use a variety of classic patterns for your buttons, and pin them to tented seating cards rather than flat cards. Consider displaying your seating cards in shallow trays filled with rice or white beans (to anchor the cards and provide a more polished look).

- **Found:** Use found papers, such as old-fashioned candy wrappers or newspaper horoscopes, and give the tables corresponding names (e.g., Bazooka, Double Bubble, Libra, Pisces). In lieu of printing seating cards, use colorful $2\frac{1}{2}$-×-$4\frac{3}{4}$-inch shipping tags and handwrite or rubber stamp guests' names.

ORGANIC MINIMAL

SIMPLE, FRESH, AND MODERN, organic minimal style combines
natural beauty with modern design. Neutral colors, clean lines, organic shapes,
and natural textures combine to provide a relaxed, comfortable air.

ORGANIC MINIMAL STYLE

PALETTES

Khaki   Off-white   Dove gray   Charcoal   Sea foam   Sage

INSPIRATION

Lotta Jansdotter, Hable Construction, Muji, Isamu Noguchi, Scandinavian Design, Pearlfisher for Jamie Oliver, Erica Tanov, Heath Ceramics

FONTS

Bosin, Pea Olson, FG Rakel, Neutra Book, Helvetica, Univers 45 Light, URW Underwood, Remington Weather

TEXTURES

Linen, burlap, glass, unfinished wood, cork, chalkboard

VENUES

Beach, winery, farm, art gallery, museum, modern/minimal hotel, botanic garden, park

DETAILS

Serve finger foods, such as sliders or doughnut holes, in natural cone coffee filters ✻ *Rent natural wood farm tables paired with bentwood or Emeco aluminum café chairs* ✻ Instead of printing individual menus, paint two to four large pieces of plywood with chalkboard paint and write your menu in chalk. Hang in a few spots at your reception, so they are visible to all guests ✻ *As a parting gift, give guests a bottle of local olive oil or wine, decorated with a personalized label or tag* ✻ Place an herb sprig on the napkin at each place setting ✻ *In lieu of favors, make a donation to a favorite environmental cause, plant trees, or purchase carbon offsets*

PUTTING IT ALL TOGETHER

1.

NATURAL LINENS
Use natural cotton burlaps and linens for table settings, napkins, and bridal attire.

2.

FARMERS' MARKET FLOWERS
Choose local, seasonal flowers for your bouquet and centerpieces.

3.

FILAMENT BULBS
If you have control over the lighting in your venue, hang simple filament bulbs over tables for your reception.

4.

SCULPTURAL CENTERPIECES
Branches and sculptural flowers make elegant, minimal centerpieces. For a more rustic feel, use dogwood, magnolias, Chinese lantern plants, or olive branches. For a more lush look, use orchids, pitcher plants, or staghorn ferns.

5.

UNEXPECTED ORGANIC DETAILS
Use coffee beans, dried cannellini beans, or black-eyed peas in shallow trays to display seating cards or programs or to surround votives in clear glass holders.

6.

ORGANIC, SEASONAL, LOCAL FOODS
Serve organic foods that are local to the region and thus have less environmental impact. Serve each course family style on large wooden platters, and consider pairing with local wines.

RSVP

MR. AND MRS. PATRICK J. MCGINNIS
REQUEST THE PLEASURE OF YOUR COMPANY
AT THE MARRIAGE OF THEIR DAUGHTER

ELIZABETH ANN
TO SIMON PETERS

SATURDAY, THE NINETEENTH OF MARCH
TWO THOUSAND AND ELEVEN
AT HALF PAST FOUR IN THE AFTERNOON

L'AUBERGE DE SEDONA
SEDONA, ARIZONA

· · · · · · · · · ·

DINNER & DANCING TO FOLLOW

BALSA WOOD INVITATIONS

LEVEL
Advanced

CATEGORY
Invitations

TIME
8 to 10 hours

WHEN TO START
14 to 18 weeks before the wedding (Invitations should be mailed 8 weeks before the wedding.)

GROUP OR INDIVIDUAL
Individual; however, it can be handy to enlist help to assemble and mail them.

. . .

- *Station 1: Address the invitation envelopes.*
- *Station 2: Affix the postage.*
- *Station 3: Collate the invitations and enclosures.*
- *Station 4: Stuff and seal the invitations.*

BUDGET
$500 (including custom stamps and supplies)

Balsa wood, available at most art supply stores, makes a lovely surface for printing and is light and sturdy enough to mail. If your invitation has several enclosures, such as a reply card, directions cards, and rehearsal-dinner invitation, cut a test piece of balsa out in each size and make sure all the pieces will fit in the envelope. If they are too snug, trim each piece down by 1/8 inch and try again.

MATERIALS

Makes 100 invitations

- Custom rubber stamps (see "Resources," page 249)
- Five 5-×-5-inch acrylic mounts
- Sixty to seventy 4-×-24-inch sheets 1/16- to 1/8-inch-thick balsa wood for invitations
- Thirty to forty 4-×-24-inch sheets 1/16- to 1/8-inch-thick balsa wood for RSVP postcards
- White and brown water-soluble printmaking ink
- 5 to 10 sheets blank text-weight printer paper
- 125 to 150 #10 top-opening envelopes
- Postage stamps for invitation and RSVP envelopes

TOOLS

- Organic Minimal Invitation templates (available online at www.chroniclebooks.com/handmade-weddings)
- Font: Univers 45 Light
- Rubber cement
- Masking tape
- Cutting mat
- Craft knife, with extra blades
- Cork-backed metal ruler
- Corner rounder (optional)
- Newsprint
- Scrap paper
- Pencil
- 2 paper plates
- Brayer (a hand-roller used in printmaking, available at art supply stores)
- Glue sticks

HOW TO

1. Customize and order your rubber stamps.

Customize and send the Organic Minimal Invitation templates to a local stamp maker or online vendor to be made into rubber stamps.

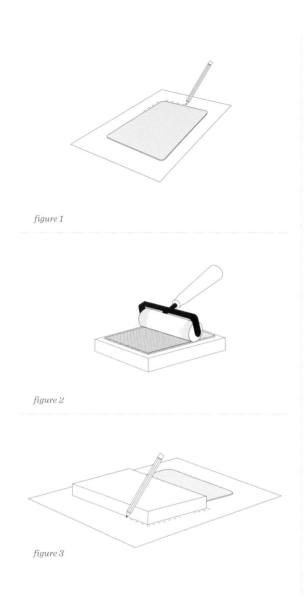

figure 1

figure 2

figure 3

Ask them to mount the stamp with no handle, as this will allow you to apply pressure over a large area using the palms of your hands. Or make your own border design by using a computer graphics program or by drawing it by hand. A rubber stamp can be made with either a hard-copy printout of your artwork or a high-resolution computer graphics file. Remember that the artwork needs to be the mirror image of what you want to stamp, so be sure to tell the stamp maker what direction you want it to face. Mount the small stamps on acrylic using rubber cement to provide a backing area that is larger than your wood, allowing you to mark the edges on your scrap paper for alignment (see step 3).

2. Trim your balsa wood.

Using masking tape, mark the width and height of your invitations and RSVP cards on your cutting mat (4-×-9 1/4-inch cards for invitations and 4-×-6-inch cards for the RSVPs). Using a craft knife and cork-backed metal ruler, trim the balsa. For each card, make several shallow vertical cuts through the wood until it is cut clean through. As soon as your blade begins to dull, put in a fresh blade. Each piece of balsa should yield four 4-×-6-inch RSVP cards and two 4-×-9 1/4-inch invitations. Use a corner rounder to round the corners if desired.

3. Make a few test prints, and print the cards.

Lay newsprint down over a 2-×-3-foot work area. Place an RSVP card face up on your scrap paper, and mark the four corners on the paper with a pencil *(figure 1)*. (We recommend starting with the RSVP card because it is the least complicated to print.) Squeeze a quarter-sized dollop of white printmaking ink onto a paper plate. Roll the brayer in the ink until it is coated evenly. Place your patterned RSVP rubber stamp faceup on your work surface, aligned with the pencil marks you just made. Roll an even coat of ink onto the stamp *(figure 2)*. Press the stamp firmly onto your RSVP card, marking the bottom two corners of the stamp on your scrap paper *(figure 3)*. Lift the stamp and observe the ink coverage and alignment. Do a few more test stamps, adjusting the amount of ink and the position of the stamp. Once you are satisfied with the result, mark the stamp placement and, using this as your guide, print the rest of your RSVP cards. Be sure to print 15 to 20 extras to allow for test prints when adding the brown layers to the front and back. Let the cards dry.

Repeat this process with the two white-patterned areas on your invitation cards. Once the white layers are complete, clean your brayer and repeat with the brown ink and remaining stamps.

4. Assemble and mail your invitations.
Affix postage to the RSVP card and invitation envelopes—remember to check the weight at your local post office in advance. Address the envelopes (see the appendix "How to Address and Assemble Your Invitations, " page 256). Collate the invitation and RSVP cards. Insert each invitation set into an envelope so that when it is pulled out with your right hand, the invitation is facing the right way up. Seal the envelopes with a glue stick.

VARIATIONS

Wood gives this invitation a natural texture that is perfect for most outdoor weddings, whether your venue is a beach, forest, park, or garden.

- **Retro Homespun:** Combine a simple invitation rubber stamped on balsa with a button-and-ribbon tie and pretty patterned envelope liner, like those used in the Retro Homespun Invitations (page 25).

- **Happy Graphic:** Print your text in bold fonts and colors, similar to those used in the Sparkle & Spin Invitations (page 103).

TALLOW-BERRY-&-COTTON-BUD BOUTONNIERES

Preserved Texas tallow berries, available year-round at floral and craft stores, have an organic shape and sturdy wooded stems that work perfectly for a boutonniere. Add cotton buds (available only in the fall—confirm with your local florist or flower market), and your boutonnieres take on a softer character. The basic technique of wrapping a boutonniere can be used for any type of material—from herb sprigs to fresh flowers, feathers, and found objects.

MATERIALS
Makes 4 to 6 boutonnieres
· 1 bunch Texas tallow berries
  (about 12 stems)
· 1 bunch cotton buds (see
  project introduction)
· Brown floral tape
· 3 yards ¼-inch ribbon or
  twill tape
· 4 to 6 corsage pins

TOOLS
· Ruler
· Scissors
· Hot glue gun and glue sticks

HOW TO
1. Bundle the berries and buds.

Arrange 3 to 4 berry and cotton bud stems into an attractive bundle. Secure in place with brown floral tape.

2. Wrap the stems.

To wrap the middle segment of the stems as shown, cut an 8-inch length of ribbon. Using hot glue, affix one end of the ribbon to a stem. Wrap the ribbon tightly around the stems several times until you are happy with its appearance. Trim the ribbon end and secure it using another dab of hot glue. Tie a short (approximately 6 inches) length of ribbon in a bow in the middle of the wrapped area.

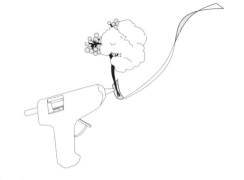

figure 1

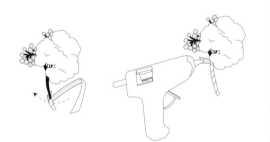

figure 2

figure 3

To wrap the entire stem from top to bottom, cut a 12-inch length of ribbon. Fold the end of the ribbon over the bottom ends of the stems, and affix into place using hot glue (*figure 1*). Wrap the ribbon tightly around the stems, covering the end of the ribbon, and continuing until you reach the berries. Trim the ribbon and secure it using another dab of hot glue (*figure 2*). Tie a short (approximately 6 inches) length of ribbon in a bow in the middle of the wrapped area (*figure 3*).

3. Finish the boutonniere.

Insert a corsage pin into the back of the boutonniere.

VARIATIONS

- **Retro Homespun:** Use colorful striped or gingham ribbon, combined with millinery flowers, acorns, or mushrooms. If your materials don't have stems, attach them to floral wire using hot glue, then wrap the floral wire stems with ribbon.

- **Modern Classic:** Use fresh flowers, enlisting your bridesmaids to create the boutonnieres on the morning of the wedding.

- **Found:** Use found objects, such as model train or dollhouse supplies, flower or bird shapes punched out of found papers, feathers, or buttons. If your materials don't have stems, attach them to floral wire using hot glue, then wrap the floral wire stems with ribbon.

PATTERNED-PAPER PROGRAMS

LEVEL

Moderate

....

CATEGORY

Ceremony

....

TIME

4 to 6 hours

....

WHEN TO START

1 to 2 weeks before
the wedding

....

**GROUP OR
INDIVIDUAL**

Group (after printing)

...

- *Station 1: Cut out the pages.*
- *Station 2: Collate.*
- *Station 3: Punch holes.*
- *Station 4: Insert the brads
  or eyelets.*

....

BUDGET

$100

These simple programs use mix-and-match patterned paper covers to create a fresh, eclectic look at your ceremony. Small brads or eyelets hold the pages together and add a clean finish.

MATERIALS

Makes 100 programs—4 pages plus cover

- Two hundred fifty 8 1/2-×-11-inch sheets white or ecru text-weight paper
- Fifteen 8 1/2-×-11-inch sheets label stock
- 225 sheets patterned paper trimmed to 6 1/4 × 4 3/4 inches
- One hundred 1/4-inch brads or 3-mm eyelets

TOOLS

- Patterned-Paper Program templates (available online at www.chroniclebooks.com/handmade-weddings)
- Fonts: Remington Weather and Bosin
- Laser or inkjet printer, with extra ink cartridges
- Craft knife, with extra blades
- Ruler
- Cutting mat
- Scrap paper
- Pencil
- 1/8-inch hole punch
- Eyelet setter (optional)

HOW TO

1. Customize and print program cover labels and interior pages.

Customize your program cover labels and interior pages using the online templates. The template for the interior pages has limited formatting and does not allow you to save your work, so you may wish to lay them out in a word processing or graphic design program instead of using the template. On a laser or inkjet printer, make a test print of the interior pages, checking the alignment of the text, front to back. Print 100 copies on the white paper. Each 8 1/2-×-11-inch sheet will yield two 6 1/4-×-4 3/4-inch interior pages. Then print the cover labels

on the label stock. Each sheet will yield eight 4-×-1-inch labels. Cut out the pages and labels along the crop marks using a craft knife, ruler, and cutting mat.

2. Assemble your programs.

Place a patterned front cover onto a piece of scrap paper and mark the bottom two corners with a pencil. Place a label on the patterned paper as you would like it to appear, approximately 1/2 inch from the bottom edge, and mark the right-hand corners. Use these marks to place your labels in the same spot every time on your program covers. Collate the covers, interior pages, and labels. Punch a hole in the top left corner of each collated program. Insert a brad or eyelet and flatten.

VARIATIONS

- **Happy Graphic:** Print or purchase three to four graphic patterned papers for your covers.

- **Modern Classic:** Use a tailored pattern for your program cover. In lieu of brads, tie a 3/8-inch satin ribbon into a square knot or bow. Or bind the spine with a 1/4-inch satin ribbon. Punch two 1/8-inch holes in the spine, approximately 3 inches apart. Thread a 12-inch ribbon through the holes, front to back. Thread them back to front into the opposite hole. Pull taut and tie a bow.

- **Found:** Use a variety of found papers for the covers, such as vintage maps, security envelopes, kraft paper, or recycled gift wrap. Combine with colorful contrasting brads.

RUBBER-STAMPED CONFETTI BAGS

LEVEL
Moderate

CATEGORY
Ceremony

TIME
4 to 6 hours

WHEN TO START
3 to 4 weeks before
the wedding

**GROUP OR
INDIVIDUAL**
You and a friend
(after stamp is created)

BUDGET
$75 to $100

Birdseed serves as a fun, biodegradable confetti substitute. Packaged in rubber-stamped cotton muslin bags, they have a pretty, organic feel.

MATERIALS
Makes 100 bags
- 4-×-4-inch Mastercarve artist's carving block
- 8-ounce tube water-based printmaking ink in brown
- One hundred ten 3-×-5-inch muslin bags
- 12-×-12-inch piece muslin, or 5 to 10 extra muslin bags with drawstrings
- Birdseed
- Five to six 8 1/2-×-11-inch sheets kraft paper

TOOLS
- Confetti Bag templates (available online at www .chroniclebooks.com/ handmade-weddings)
- Tracing paper
- Pencil
- Ballpoint pen
- U- and V-shaped linoleum block carving tools
- Rubber cement (optional)
- Acrylic mount, slightly larger than the carving block (optional)
- 2 or 3 sheets newsprint
- Paper plate
- Brayer (a hand-roller used in printmaking, available at art supply stores)
- Inkjet or laser printer
- Craft knife
- Ruler
- Cutting mat
- 1/8-inch hole punch

HOW TO:
1. Make your pattern.

Trace the templates provided onto tracing paper with a pencil. Or find a pattern you want to reproduce, or draw your own. If you are

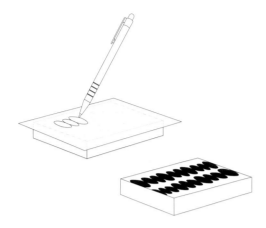

figure 1

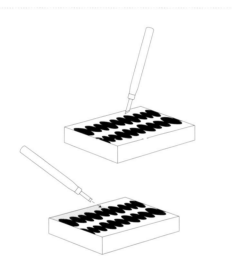

figure 2

figure 3

using a pattern, you will need to reverse the pattern so that it comes out correctly. Trace the pattern onto tracing
paper, flip the paper over, and trace the image again. (Alternatively, if you have access to a scanner, scan the artwork and flip it using photo-editing software. Print and trace.)

2. Transfer the artwork onto your carving block.

Place the tracing paper facedown over the rubber carving block. Trace over the pattern with a ballpoint pen to transfer the graphite of the pencil onto the block. Remove the tracing paper. Retrace the pattern on the block in pen. Color in all the areas that will be stamped onto the paper *(figure 1)*.

3. Carve out the pattern.

Carve out the blank areas of the block *(figure 2)*. Carve around the outer edge of the image with a knife, then cut toward the image with the U-tool. If desired, spread rubber cement onto the back of the block, and affix it to the acrylic mount. Let dry.

4. Stamp the muslin bags.

Lay newsprint down on a 3-×-3-foot work surface. Spread a quarter-sized dollop of ink on your paper plate. Roll your brayer in the ink, then roll an even layer of ink onto the rubber stamp *(figure 3)*. Do some test stamps onto a scrap or spare muslin bag. (Because the print will look different depending on what type of surface is used, it is important to do your test print on muslin or a similar material.) If needed, refine your carving. When you are happy with the print, begin stamping your muslin bags *(figure 4)*. Set aside your first print as a reference for color consistency. Continue stamping, adding more ink to your stamp as needed. Let dry.

5. Print tags and fill the bags with birdseed.

Customize and print the Confetti Tag templates online. Print onto kraft paper using an inkjet or laser printer. Trim tags along the crop marks provided using a craft knife, ruler, and cutting mat. Punch a hole about 1/4 inch from the end of each tag.

Fill the bags with birdseed. Thread the tag through one of the drawstrings, pull the drawstrings taut, and tie in a bow.

VARIATIONS

Adjust the look of these bags by choosing a different pattern and by replacing the drawstrings with a coordinating ribbon. Cut the drawstrings, pull out, and use a large needle, such as a yarn needle, to thread the new ribbon.

- **Retro Homespun:** Stamp your design in red or orange ink. Consider replacing the bags' drawstrings with 1/8-inch gingham or striped or twill ribbon.

- **Girly Romantic:** In lieu of birdseed, fill the bags with biodegradable confetti, lavender, or flower petals. If desired, replace the bags' drawstrings with 1/4-inch seam tape.

- **Modern Classic:** Stamp your design in black ink, and fill the bags with biodegradable confetti, available in a range of colors. Replace the bags' drawstrings with 1/8- or 1/4-inch satin ribbon.

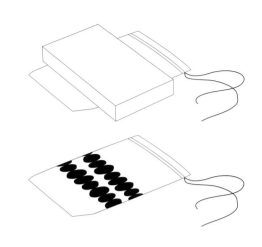

figure 4

CHALKBOARD-PAINT TABLE NUMBERS

5

Bottles, jars, flower pots, or vases spray painted with chalkboard paint are perfect vehicles for table numbers, and they double as vessels for flowers. Chalk is forgiving, so feel free to use your creativity in handwriting your table numbers or names.

LEVEL
Easy

CATEGORY
Reception

TIME
3 to 4 hours

WHEN TO START
2 to 4 weeks before
the wedding

**GROUP OR
INDIVIDUAL**
You and a friend
(Each person spray
paints half of the vessels.
Once they dry, handwrite
the table numbers on
your own.)

BUDGET
$20 to $50 depending
on types of vessels used

MATERIALS
Makes 10 table numbers
- 10 vessels with a smooth surface: vases, wine bottles, large glass jars, or cans
- 2 to 3 cans chalkboard spray paint
- Chalk

TOOLS
- 10 to 12 sheets newspaper, or a drop cloth
- Medium-sized cardboard box, about as tall as your tallest vessel
- Rubber gloves
- Face mask
- Sponge

HOW TO

1. Set up your spray booth and drying areas.
In a well-ventilated area or outdoors, lay down newspaper or a drop cloth two to three times the size of your cardboard box. This will be your spray booth. If you've enlisted a friend to help, set up a second spray booth. In a separate area, cover a 3-×-3-foot work surface with newspaper. This will be your drying area.

2. Paint the vessels.
Wearing rubber gloves and a face mask, place a vessel in your cardboard box. Spray it with chalkboard paint, tilting and rotating the vessel as you go to get an even coat of paint. Set it aside to dry. Apply a second touch-up coat if needed. Repeat for all vessels.

3. Write the table numbers.

Condition the chalkboard paint on each vessel by rubbing chalk all over it, then rubbing it off with a damp sponge. Once dry, write the table numbers or names on each vessel using chalk.

Or, to use regular vessels and stencil the table numbers onto balsa:

For each table number, you'll need:
- One 4-×-6-inch piece balsa wood
- Laser or inkjet printer, with extra ink cartridges
- Pencil
- Freezer paper
- Craft knife, with extra blades
- Ruler
- Cutting mat
- Chalkboard spray paint
- One 1/4-inch wooden dowel, 8 to 12 inches long (depending on the size of your vessel)
- Hot glue gun and glue sticks

Print your numbers on an inkjet printer and trace onto freezer paper. Cut out each number using a craft knife, ruler, and cutting mat to create a stencil. Lay the freezer-paper stencil over the wood, and spray paint. Let dry completely, and peel the stencil away carefully. If desired, cut off the corners of the balsa wood. Hot glue the wooden dowel to the back of the balsa wood.

VARIATIONS

Colored chalkboard paint, available at select hardware stores, makes this project adaptable to many different styles and palettes. You can also make your own following the simple instructions below. You will need:

- Bucket or container, for mixing
- Unsanded tile grout
- Colored latex-based paint
- Paint stirrer
- Paint brush
- Sandpaper

Mix 2 tablespoons of unsanded tile grout per 1 cup of paint, stirring with your paint stirrer. Paint the chalkboard paint onto your vessels. Once dry, sand the vessels with sandpaper.

- **Girly Romantic:** Consider using pale pink paint. Or write your table numbers in script or calligraphy.

- **Happy Graphic:** Use bright red, yellow, cobalt blue, or gray paint. If desired, use a different color for each table, and color code the table numbers and escort cards, too.

- **Found:** Use found and recycled vessels, such as recycled detergent bottles, olive oil cans, large jars, or milk jugs (cut a larger opening if needed with scissors or a can opener).

KRAFT PAPER MENUS

6

LEVEL
Easy

CATEGORY
Reception

TIME
3 to 4 hours

WHEN TO START
2 to 3 weeks before
the wedding

**GROUP OR
INDIVIDUAL**
Individual

BUDGET
$30

These simple menus, printed on recycled kraft paper and clipped to your guests' napkins with tiny clothespins, are the perfect way to add an understated bistro feel to your wedding.

MATERIALS
Makes 100 menus
- One hundred 8 1/2-×-11-inch sheets text-weight kraft paper (such as Greengrocer Brown Bag Paper by Leader Paper Products)
- One hundred 1-inch-long mini clothespins

TOOLS
- Kraft Paper Menu template (available online at www .chroniclebooks.com/ handmade-weddings)
- Font: Bosin
- Laser or inkjet printer, with extra ink cartridges
- Craft knife
- Ruler
- Cutting mat

HOW TO

1. Lay out and print your menus.

Customize your menu using the online template. Print 100 copies on your kraft paper using a laser or inkjet printer. Trim at the crop marks using a craft knife, ruler, and cutting mat.

2. Clip your menus to the napkins.

Fold a napkin into a rectangular shape (for most standard napkins, fold into thirds, then fold in half). Clip the menu at a slight angle to the napkin with a mini clothespin. Repeat to assemble the desired number.

VARIATIONS

- **Retro Homespun:** Clip the menus to handmade mix-and-match fabric napkins; follow instructions for the Mix-&-Match Pocket Squares (page 37) but measure to 18 x 18 inches.

- **Girly Romantic:** Consider spray painting the clothespins gold or silver. Use script or calligraphy fonts for the menu.

- **Happy Graphic:** Spray paint the clothespins a bright color, and use an upbeat, modern font for the menu.

TERRARIUM PLACE CARDS & FAVORS

7

These terrarium favors can be made in many shapes and sizes, and even serve as centerpieces, but we love the small fishbowl variety, filled with tiny succulents, ferns, or herbs. They can also double as either place cards or seating cards with the addition of a jumbo craft stick dipped in chalkboard paint.

LEVEL
Easy

CATEGORY
Reception

TIME
20 to 30 minutes
per favor

WHEN TO START
2 to 3 days before
the wedding

**GROUP OR
INDIVIDUAL**
Group

· · ·

- *Station 1: Lay down stones.*
- *Station 2: Arrange the plants.*
- *Station 3: Wipe down and tidy the bowls.*
- *Station 4: Dip craft sticks.*

BUDGET
$5 to $6
per terrarium

MATERIALS
Makes 100 favors and place cards

- Four to five 50-pound bags of pebbles
- One hundred 3 1/4-inch glass fishbowl vases
- 1 bag sand, or potting soil
- 3 to 5 small plants per terrarium: we recommend small succulents or cacti, small ferns, or herbs such as parsley, mint, or rosemary
- 1 pint chalkboard paint
- 125 jumbo (6-inch) craft sticks

TOOLS

- Clean cloth or rag
- Ruler
- Plastic container, at least 5 inches deep (a large yogurt container works well)
- Sharpie, or a piece of masking tape
- Clothesline and clothespins
- Drop cloth or newspaper
- Chalk, or a white gel pen
- Damp cloth or sponge

HOW TO

1. Place the stones.

Place a layer of pebbles, about 1/2 inch deep, in the bottom of your glass bowls.

2. Place your sand or potting soil and arrange your plants.

If you are using succulents, place a layer of sand, about 1/2 inch deep, in each terrarium and arrange your plants in a pleasing manner; we recommend 3 to 5 plants per terrarium, but adjust according to the size of your container. If you are using ferns or other plants, use potting soil instead of sand.

3. Place the pebbles.

Place a layer of small pebbles, about 1/2 inch deep, around the base of your plants.

4. Tidy up your terrariums.

Using a cloth, wipe away any stray dirt from the sides of the bowls.

5. Add your markers.

You can transform your terrariums into favors that double as either a seating card or place card. Measure 4 inches from the bottom of your plastic container, and mark the spot with a Sharpie or piece of masking tape. Pour chalkboard paint into your container until it reaches the mark. Set up your clothesline, placing a drop cloth or newspaper below it to catch dripping paint. Dip your craft sticks in the paint until they touch the bottom of the container, and immediately clip them to your clothesline, paint-side down. Let them dry. Once dry, rub one side of each painted stick with chalk, and wipe it off with a damp cloth or sponge. This will prime the area. Let them dry. Once the surface is dry, write each guest's name in chalk on a stick and insert the unpainted end of the stick into your terrarium. (If you are having trouble writing in a small scale with chalk, a white gel pen works well, too.)

VARIATIONS

Terrariums can be made out of virtually any vessel, and a wide variety of plants, from green foliage to flowering plants, can be used.

- **Retro Homespun:** Instead of glass bowls, use jam jars (such as Bonne Maman jars with gingham lids), Mason jars, or teacups. Consider adding small decorations, such as millinery birds or mushrooms, or whimsical cupcake toppers.

- **Girly Romantic:** Make your terrariums in apothecary jars or Bell jars, available from many floral and craft stores. Choose romantic plants and flowers, such as lavender, and embellish with vintage-inspired found objects, such as millinery birds, shells, or silk butterflies.

- **Found:** Make your terrariums using recycled/found vessels, such as beakers, glass milk bottles, glass yogurt containers, or jam jars.

STENCILED TABLE RUNNER

This table runner uses freezer paper, a plastic-coated kraft paper typically used to wrap frozen foods, to make stencils for decorating. Because of its plastic surface, freezer paper sticks temporarily to fabric when it is ironed, making it easy to work with and reposition if needed. Make one table runner per table if time allows (you'll need to cut out a separate stencil for each number), or just make one for the head table. It'll make a lovely keepsake after the wedding.

LEVEL
Advanced

CATEGORY
Reception

TIME
2 to 3 hours

WHEN TO START
4 to 6 weeks before
the wedding

**GROUP OR
INDIVIDUAL**
Individual

BUDGET
$50 to $75

MATERIALS
Makes one 18-×-10-foot table runner

- 3 1/2 yards linen
- Two 18-×-32-inch pieces freezer paper, plus two 6-×-6-inch pieces freezer paper for test prints (available at most supermarkets)
- Acrylic fabric ink in brown
- 3 sheets blank text-weight printer paper
- Matching thread

TOOLS

- Stenciled Table Runner template (available online at www.chroniclebooks.com/handmade-weddings)
- Iron and ironing board
- Rotary cutter
- Ruler
- Cutting mat
- Craft knife, with extra blades
- Pencil
- Newsprint
- Paper plate or artist's palette
- Plastic spoon
- Paper towel
- Stencil brush
- Masking tape
- Clear tape
- Scissors
- Press cloth or dishcloth
- Straight pins
- Sewing machine

HOW TO

1. Wash, iron, and cut your fabric.

Wash your fabric to allow for shrinkage. Iron it flat. Check the measurements of your tables, and adjust the measurements of your table runner accordingly. Typically, the width of a table runner is about 18 inches, but it can be adjusted depending on how much of the table you wish to cover. The ends of the runner should hang at least 6 inches below the edge of the table. Using a rotary cutter, ruler, and cutting mat, cut out a piece of fabric that measures 2 inches longer and 2 inches wider than your finished runners. The extra fabric will be used to sew a 1-inch hem on all sides of your runner.

2. Make a test stencil.

Using your craft knife and cutting mat, cut out a few simple shapes (any shape will do) from the center of your 6-×-6-inch scraps of freezer paper. If the paper begins to tear, put a fresh blade in your craft knife.

Set your iron to medium-high. Lay your test fabric on your ironing board. Lay your test stencil, plastic-side down, on top of your test fabric. Place your press cloth or dishcloth over the stencil and iron on medium-high in a smooth, continuous motion, so as to avoid tearing the stencil. If an air bubble appears in the stencil, lift the edge of the stencil and then smooth it back down, pushing the air out, and iron over the area again.

3. Make a test print.

Cover an approximately 3-×-3-foot work surface with newsprint for printing. Scoop or squeeze a spoonful of ink onto your paper plate or artist's palette.

Fold a paper towel in quarters. Dip your stencil brush in your ink. Gently tap the brush ends on the folded paper towel several times until most of the excess ink has been removed. This ensures that the brush is not overloaded with ink, which can cause the ink to seep under your stencil, resulting in a messy print. When loaded with the proper amount of ink, the brush will transfer a thin, even layer of ink to your stencil, resulting in crisp outlines.

To apply the ink to your test stencil, use a technique called stippling. Blot the brush over the area you wish to print in a quick, repeated up-and-down motion (*figure 1, page 158*). This will transfer a thin, evenly blended layer of ink over your fabric. Let it dry. Add another layer of ink in the same fashion. Continue to add layers until you have achieved a solid area of color, loading your brush with more ink as needed and letting the fabric dry between each layer.

Once the paint is completely dry, carefully remove the stencil. If the ink seeped under the stencil, or is not dark enough, practice your technique on another test stencil.

4. Cut out your stencils.

Print the Stenciled Table Runner template onto three pieces of 8 1/2-×-11-inch paper. Lay your 18-×-32-inch pieces of freezer paper on your cutting mat, one directly on top of the other, plastic sides down. Secure them to your cutting mat on two sides with small strips of masking tape. Align the three sections of the template and join them with clear tape. Trim off any excess paper using scissors. Lay the artwork on top of the freezer paper, faceup, and secure it to the cutting mat on two sides with small strips of masking tape. If your cutting mat is small, you may wish to cut one section of the template at a time.

Carefully cut out the shaded areas of the stencil with your craft knife, making clean cuts through the artwork and both pieces of freezer paper and replacing your blade frequently (*figure 2, page 158*).

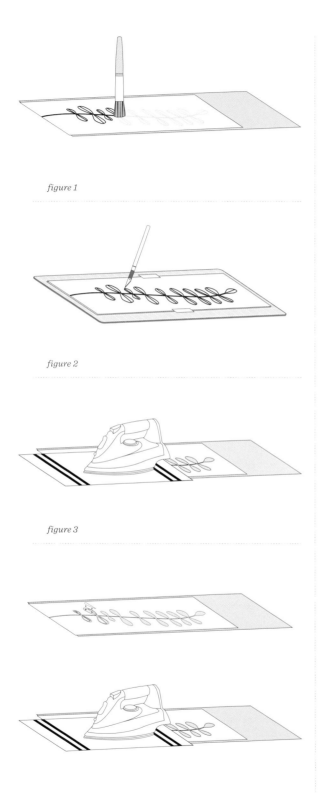

figure 1

figure 2

figure 3

figure 4

If you make a mistake and accidentally cut past the shaded area, don't worry—you can rejoin the cut when you iron the freezer paper to your fabric. Save any loose pieces of the stencil, such as the interior sections of the leaves. Number each leaf and its corresponding loose pieces so that you can piece them back together when you attach your stencils (step 5).

5. Attach your stencils.

Position your first stencil on the runner, excluding any loose pieces. When you are happy with its placement, secure it with two pieces of masking tape. This will keep the stencil from moving when you iron it.

Lay your fabric on your ironing board. Place a press cloth or dishcloth over the stencil and iron on medium-high, moving your iron in a smooth, continuous motion *(figure 3)*. Check to make sure all parts of the stencil are fused to the fabric; if they are not attaching, increase the heat slightly or iron over the problem areas again (or both).

Position any loose pieces of the stencil, such as the interiors of the leaves *(figure 4)*. Repeat step 5 to secure the loose pieces. Repeat step 5 again for the second stencil on the other side of your runner.

6. Print your stencils.

Lay one end of your runner on your newsprint-covered printing area. Apply ink to the stencil brush, using the blotting and stippling technique you practiced in step 3. Let the paint dry completely, and then carefully peel off the freezer paper. Repeat on the other side of your runner. Iron the dry fabric on high heat; this will set the ink and make it washable after use.

7. Hem your runner.

Make a ½-inch fold along all four sides of the wrong side of your runner, pinning the fold into place using straight pins. Using a sewing machine, sew the hems using a running stitch and matching thread. When you are done, trim the thread and remove the pins. Iron the hems.

VARIATIONS

Runners can be made out of many fabrics. Cottons and linens are best, while heavy fabrics like denim and canvas should be avoided as they don't tend to lay flat. You can use your own artwork in place of the template. Remember that the center of the runner is most likely going to be covered with your centerpiece and serving platters, so concentrate on designs for the ends.

- **Modern Classic:** Sew a plain black or pale pink runner. Stencil clip-art calligraphy flourishes or your monogram (or both) at either end.

- **Found:** In lieu of fabric, use rolled kraft paper for your runners. Because freezer paper may stick to the kraft paper (do a test to check), use medium-weight (3 to 7 mil) tinted Mylar. Cut out your Mylar stencil with a craft knife, position it on your runner, and secure it on two sides with masking tape. Cover any areas that you don't want to paint with newsprint, and apply a light coat of spray paint to the area that you want to print. Spray paint is less likely than brushed paints to seep under the stencil. Once dry, carefully remove the masking tape and stencil.

TEST-TUBE FAVORS

Test tubes make elegant, inexpensive vessels for favors such as teas, hard candies, herbs, or flavored salts. A pretty rubber-stamped fabric tag tells guests what's inside.

LEVEL
Easy

CATEGORY
Favors and gifts

TIME
6 to 8 hours

WHEN TO START
1 to 2 weeks before
the wedding

**GROUP OR
INDIVIDUAL**
Group

- *Station 1: Trim the tags.*
- *Station 2: Punch the holes.*
- *Station 3: Fill the test tubes and insert corks.*
- *Station 4: Attach the tags.*

BUDGET
$50 to $75

MATERIALS
Makes 100 favors
- 1 yard muslin or lightweight canvas
- One hundred 18-×-150-mm glass rimless test tubes with corks
- Approximately 4 ounces (50 cups) loose tea, candy, herbs, or flavored salts (we recommend staying away from liquids)
- Brown ink pad
- One hundred 3-mm gray eyelets
- 100-foot length thin yarn or twine

TOOLS
- Favor Tag template (available online at www.chroniclebooks .com/handmade-weddings)
- Font: Remington Weather
- Rotary cutter
- Ruler
- Cutting mat
- 1/8-inch hole punch
- Eyelet setter (available at craft supply stores such as Paper Source, www.paper-source.com)

HOW TO

1. Customize and order your favor tag stamps.

Customize and send the Favor Tag template to a local stamp maker or online vendor to be made into rubber stamps. Or make your own design by using a computer graphics program or drawing it by hand. A rubber stamp can be made with either a hard-copy printout of your artwork or a high-resolution computer graphics file. Remember that the artwork needs to be the mirror image of what you want to stamp, so be sure to tell the stamp maker what direction you want it to face.

2. Trim and stamp your tags.

Using a rotary cutter, ruler, and cutting mat, cut your fabric into 3/4-×-3 1/2-inch strips. Fray the edges on one short side. Blot your rubber stamp onto your ink pad, and stamp your strips with the right-hand side of the stamp text aligning with the fringe side of the tag. Punch a 1/8-inch hole on the left-hand side of each tag, about 1/2 inch from the edge. Insert the eyelet and fasten using your eyelet setter per the manufacturer's instructions.

3. Fill the tubes and affix the tags.

Fill the washed and dried test tubes with your favor material, and insert the corks. For each test tube, cut a 12-inch length of yarn or twine. Wrap it around the tube two to three times, and then thread the ends through the eyelet and tie in a bow.

VARIATIONS

- **Happy Graphic:** Instead of corks, use brightly colored test tube caps (available in red, yellow, orange, cobalt blue, and green from scientific equipment suppliers). Fill your test tubes with colorful graphic candies, such as Red Hots, lemon drops, or gumballs.

- **Found:** In lieu of fabric, print your tags from scraps of patterned paper.

NOTES

MODERN CLASSIC

SIMPLE AND CHIC, modern classic weddings draw from iconic
sources of inspiration, from Coco Chanel to Kate Spade. Clean lines, classic
patterns, and crisp colors interact to create a tailored, timeless look.

MODERN CLASSIC STYLE

PALETTES

Black

White

Pale pink

Pale blue

Pale Yellow

Fuchsia
(just a hint of)

INSPIRATION

Coco Chanel, Grace Kelly, Jacqueline Kennedy, James Bond, *Breakfast at Tiffany's*, Hollywood Regency, Kate Spade, J. Crew, vintage ribbon work, House of Nines Design

FONTS

Bickham, Lucia, Compendium, Copperplate Light, Engraver's Gothic Western, Classic Roman Standard Light, Mrs. Eaves Roman and Small Caps, Nelly Script

TEXTURES

Satin, grosgrain, crepe paper, patent leather, pearls, tailored bows, pleats, engraving, calligraphy, simple stripes

VENUES

Historic hotel or landmark, ballroom, penthouse loft, vineyard, private estate

DETAILS

Rent a classic car for your getaway ✳ *Take a cue from English weddings and have your bridal party wear small decorative hats or headbands* ✳ Display your centerpieces in silver urns or vessels ✳ *Incorporate black and white anemones into your floral arrangements* ✳ Wrap your bouquet in silk satin ribbon fastened with pearl pins ✳ *Have a cigar bar at your reception, coupled with a whiskey tasting bar*

PUTTING IT ALL TOGETHER

1.

TAILORED FLORAL ARRANGEMENTS

Choose classic flowers such as French tulips, roses, hydrangeas, anemones, lilacs, and sweet peas. Place them into clean, tailored arrangements.

2.

CUSTOM MONOGRAM

Have a monogram custom designed and incorporate it into your stationery and other day-of details.

3.

BREAKFAST AT TIFFANY'S

Think Audrey Hepburn when choosing attire. Wear white cocktail gloves and pearls; have your bridesmaids wear tailored cocktail dresses; dress your groomsmen in black tie.

4.

ELEGANT PARTY RENTALS

Take advantage of classic party rental furniture, including black and white Chiavari chairs with ivory, black, or pale pink cushions, and crisp black and white linens.

5.

CLASSIC COCKTAILS

Serve classic cocktails such as bourbon, martinis, or mint juleps. Add live big band or swing music to create a swank, club-like feel.

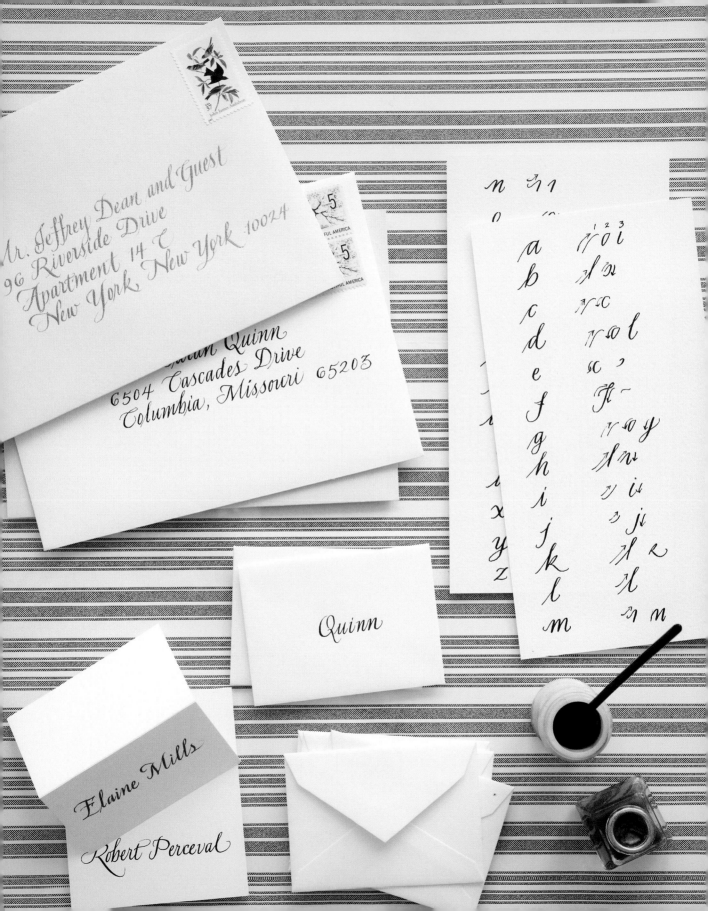

CALLIGRAPHY

with Michele Papineau,
Papineau Calligraphy

1

LEVEL
Moderate

CATEGORY
Invitations

TIME
1 to 2 hours per week,
over 6 to 8 weeks

WHEN TO START
4 to 6 months
before the wedding

**GROUP OR
INDIVIDUAL**
Individual

BUDGET
$15 to $20
(excluding paper
and envelopes)

It's amazing how simple calligraphy can be—it just takes a lot of practice! Once you get the hang of it, you can add a decorative touch to everything from invitations to seating cards and signage. Start practicing early, and most importantly, relax and take it slow—one letter at a time.

MATERIALS
- Pen nib (we recommend Gillott or Hunt)
- Pointed pen holder
- Ink
- Paper
- Sheet of blank card stock, at least 5 × 7 inches
- Envelopes

TOOLS
- Ruler
- Cutting Mat
- Craft knife, or scissors
- Pencil
- Sharpie
- Tracing paper (optional)
- Light box (optional)

HOW TO

1. Practice, practice, practice!

Attach the pen nib to the pen holder. Dip the nib in ink, hold the pen loosely, relax, and begin writing, following the letterforms shown on the next pages. Place pressure on the pen in the downward strokes, and lighten the pressure on the upward strokes. This creates the thick- and thin-line characteristic of calligraphy.

Tip: Keep the death grip off the pen. Although you should follow the letter forms initially, don't get hung up on making each letter perfect—put "yourself" into it!

2. Address your envelopes.

By hand: Measure your envelope. Using a ruler, cutting mat, and craft knife or scissors, trim your card stock so that it just fits inside your envelope (about 1/8 inch smaller on all sides). With a ruler and pencil, measure and mark a series of centered (top-to-bottom,

1 2 3 4 5 6 7 8 9 10

Now join the letters all together
abcdefghijklmnopqrstuvwxyz

A B C D E F G H I J K L M N
O P Q R S T U V W X Y Z
a b c d e f g h i j k l m n o p q r s t u v w x y z

Optional Flourishes

A B C D E F G H I J K L
M N O P Q R S T U V W X Y Z
L g h j k L L Y Z

and left-to-right) horizontal lines on the card stock indicating the bottom and top of each line of text, as well as the line spaces in between them. We recommend about a 1/2-inch line height and 1/4-inch line spaces. Most names and addresses can be written on three to four lines. Trace over your lines using your ruler and a Sharpie. This will ensure that the lines are bold enough to show through the front of your envelope.

Place your lined card inside your envelope, lines facing front. Use the lines to guide you as you write your addresses. If your addresses are of varying lengths, consider making several template cards so that your text is always centered. For example, make a three-line address card, a four-line address card, and a five-line address card.

Or using a light box: A light box allows you to draw one template and adjust the placement of your envelope so the template is always positioned where you want it to be.

With a ruler and pencil on tracing paper, measure and mark a series of horizontal lines indicating the bottom and top of each line of text, as well as the line spaces in between them. We recommend about a 1/2-inch line height and 1/4-inch line spaces. Draw as many lines of text as you think you may need. With the aid of the light box, the pencil marks will be dark enough to see through the front of your envelope.

Place the tracing-paper template on the light box. Center your envelope over it, flap open, and adjust the position until you are happy with the placement of the lines given the length of the address you are about to write. Address your envelope. Repeat for the rest of the addresses.

MR. AND MRS. JAMES BENNETT LEWIS
REQUEST THE PLEASURE OF YOUR COMPANY
AT THE MARRIAGE OF THEIR DAUGHTER

CHARLOTTE HOPE

TO

ROBERT OWEN MAYFAIR

SATURDAY, THE THIRD OF DECEMBER
TWO THOUSAND AND ELEVEN
AT FIVE O'CLOCK IN THE EVENING

BARR MANSION
AUSTIN, TEXAS

DINNER & DANCING TO FOLLOW

· KINDLY REPLY ·
BY THE FIRST OF NOVEMBER

M

ACCEPTS WITH PLEASURE

DECLINES WITH REGRET

MR. AND MRS. JAMES BENNETT LEWIS
REQUEST THE PLEASURE OF YOUR COMPANY
AT THE MARRIAGE OF THEIR DAUGHTER

CHARLOTTE HOPE

TO

ROBERT OWEN MAYFAIR

SATURDAY, THE THIRD OF DECEMBER
TWO THOUSAND AND ELEVEN
AT FIVE O'CLOCK IN THE EVENING

BARR MANSION
AUSTIN, TEXAS

DINNER & DANCING TO FOLLOW

M

ACCEPTS WITH PLEASURE   DECLINES WITH REGRET

MODERN CLASSIC INVITATIONS

This invitation suite uses a wide ribbon, sandwiched between the invitation and a backing card, to create an elegant band for keeping enclosures, such as a reply set or directions card, close at hand. A Xyron machine, which turns any type of paper into a label, makes quick work of adding a decorative layer to any of the cards in your ensemble, if desired.

LEVEL
Moderate

CATEGORY
Invitations

TIME
Printing—4 hours
Assembly—6 to 8 hours

WHEN TO START
12 weeks before
the wedding (Invitations
should be mailed 8 weeks
before the wedding.)

**GROUP OR
INDIVIDUAL**
Group (after printing)

· · ·

- *Station 1: Trim the cards.*
- *Station 2: Trim the backings.*
- *Station 3: Attach the invitation, ribbon, and backing.*
- *Station 4: Affix postage to the envelopes.*
- *Station 5: Collate the enclosures with the invitation.*
- *Station 6: Stuff and seal the envelopes.*

BUDGET
$250
(excluding postage)

MATERIALS
Makes 100 invitations
- Sixty 8 1/2-×-11-inch sheets ecru or white card stock for invitations
- Thirty 8 1/2-×-11-inch sheets ecru or white card stock for RSVP cards
- Sixty 8 1/2-×-11-inch sheets pale pink card stock for the backings
- 25 yards 1 1/2- to 2-inch satin ribbon
- One hundred twenty-five 4-bar envelopes
- One hundred twenty-five A7 envelopes
- Postage stamps for RSVP card and invitation envelopes

TOOLS
- Modern Classic Invitation template (available online at www.chroniclebooks.com/handmade-weddings)
- Font: Engraver's Gothic Western
- Inkjet printer, with extra ink cartridges
- Craft knife, with extra blades
- Ruler
- Cutting mat
- Scissors
- Double-sided tape gun and extra tape (we recommend the 3M Scotch ATG 700 Transfer Tape Dispenser)
- Bone folder
- Glue sticks, or envelope moistener with adhesive

Note: If assembling invitations with a group, be sure to have enough craft knives, rulers, cutting mats, and glue sticks on hand—we recommend four to six of each.

HOW TO
1. Print your invitations and RSVP cards.
Customize your invitation text using the online template and print 60 copies on the card stock using an inkjet printer; each copy will yield two invitations. Print 30 copies of the RSVP card on the card

stock; each copy will yield four cards. If desired, print the invitation envelope flaps and RSVP envelope faces. Because it can be tricky to feed envelopes through a home printer, you can also get a custom rubber stamp(s) made for the envelopes (see "Resources," page 249).

2. Cut out your invitations and RSVP cards.

Using a craft knife, ruler, and cutting mat or a paper cutter, cut the invitations and RSVP cards along the crop marks provided. If using a craft knife, as soon as your blade begins to dull, put in a fresh blade.

3. Trim your backing cards.

Using a craft knife, ruler, and cutting mat, cut your pink card stock into 5-×-7-inch rectangles. Each sheet of paper should yield two backing cards;

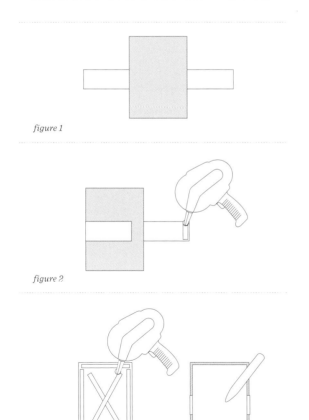

figure 1

figure 2

figure 3

cut ten to twenty extras for inevitable mistakes when assembling your invitations. They should be 1/4 inch larger than your invitations and fit into your invitation envelopes.

4. Attach your backing cards and ribbon.

Cut your ribbon into 8-inch lengths. Lay a piece of ribbon, right-side down, crosswise on your work surface. Center a backing card on it, from top to bottom and from left to right, with the back of the card facing down *(figure 1)*. Fold the ribbon ends toward the center of the card. Using a double-sided tape gun, attach the ribbon ends to the card, pulling each side taut so the ribbon lays flat *(figure 2)*. Place an invitation facedown on your work surface and apply double-sided tape to all four edges, and make an X in the middle. Or, run your invitiation through a Xyron machine. Center the invitation onto the backing card and press down. Smooth with a bone folder *(figure 3)*. Repeat for all your invitations.

5. Assemble your invitations.

If you are rubber stamping your envelopes, stamp your RSVP and return address using a custom stamp and ink pad. Affix postage to your RSVP and invitation envelopes. Collate your enclosures so that the smallest one is facing out, and slip them into the ribbon band on the back of your invitations. Insert each invitation set into an envelope so that when it is pulled out with your right hand, the invitation is facing the right way up. Seal the envelopes with a glue stick or envelope moistener.

VARIATIONS

- **Retro Homespun:** Back your invitation with fabric, and choose a pretty grosgrain or gingham ribbon for the band.

- **Organic Minimal:** Back your invitation with linen. Wrap thin twine or yarn around the backing several times, and tie a small knot to secure it.

SILHOUETTE BRIDE & GROOM SIGNS

LEVEL
Moderate

....

CATEGORY
Décor

....

TIME
3 to 4 hours

....

WHEN TO START
3 to 4 weeks before
the wedding

....

**GROUP OR
INDIVIDUAL**
Individual

....

BUDGET
$20 to $30

These boy and girl silhouettes, based on the bride and groom, give your powder rooms an elegant look, and can also be used to decorate the entrance to the ceremony venue. Remember to only include as much detail in the silhouette as you have the time and patience to cut out.

MATERIALS
Makes 2 signs
- Two to four 8 1/2-×-11-inch sheets pale pink paper
- Two 4-×-4-inch squares black foam core (optional)
- Two to four 8 1/2-×-11-inch sheets patterned paper in two different patterns
- Photographs of the bride and groom in profile
- Four to six 8 1/2-×-11-inch sheets black construction paper
- 2 yards 1/2-inch ribbon

TOOLS
- Photo-editing software and a printer, or a photocopier
- Oval templates (available online at www.chroniclebooks.com/ handmade-weddings)
- Pencil
- Tracing paper, or photocopier
- Drafting tape
- Scissors
- Craft knife, with extra blades
- Cutting mat
- Spray adhesive, or a glue stick
- Bone folder
- Hole punch (optional)
- 2 removable adhesive foam mounting squares, or double-sided tape or over-the-door hooks (optional)

HOW TO

1. Cut out your ovals.

Using a pencil, trace the Large Oval template onto tracing paper, or make a photocopy. Lay the tracing paper over your black construction paper, secure on two sides with drafting tape, and cut out with scissors. Repeat with the medium oval template and pale pink paper, and the small oval template and patterned paper.

2. Make your silhouettes.

For each photo, trace the Silhouette Oval template onto tracing paper. Using photo-editing software or a photocopier, scale your photograph so that your silhouette fits into the small oval. It should measure about 9 inches tall from the top of the head to the collar line, and 6 inches wide at the widest point. Lay the traced Silhouette Oval template over your printed photo to check the size, and adjust the photo accordingly. When you are satisfied with the size of the photo, position the traced Silhouette Oval template over your photo, securing it with drafting tape. Using a pencil, trace the portion of the silhouette that is inside the oval. Simplify details, such as tufts of hair, that will be difficult to cut out later.

Lay your traced silhouette on top of a sheet of black construction paper, and secure it with drafting tape on two sides. Using a craft knife and cutting mat or scissors, carefully cut out the silhouette, replacing your blade as soon as it begins to dull.

3. Assemble your signs.

For each sign, lay your silhouette oval right-side down on your work surface. Lay your small patterned oval, right-side up, nearby. Apply adhesive to the back of the silhouette. Turn it over and position it over your small patterned oval so that a 1/8-inch border is revealed along the bottom edge. Press down and smooth it, concentrating on the edges of the silhouette, with a bone folder. Let it dry.

Place your patterned oval and silhouette facedown on your work surface. Apply adhesive to the back of the oval. Turn it over and position it over your medium pink oval so that a 1/8-inch pink border is revealed around the entire oval. Press down and smooth it, concentrating on the edges of the patterned oval, with a bone folder. Let it dry. Repeat for your large black oval, this time allowing a 1/4 inch

black border to be revealed. Optional: For each sign, cut a 4-×-4-inch square of black foam core and affix it to the back of the sign with the adhesive. This will lift your signs off the wall slightly when they are hung, giving added dimension.

4. Prepare your signs for hanging.

Decide how the signs will be hung. If hanging from a nail, punch a hole at the top of each oval. Cut your ribbon into two 1-yard lengths. Thread a yard of ribbon through each hole, back to front. Tie the ribbon into a bow for hanging, and trim the ends (fold the ribbon end in half and cut the fold at a 45-degree angle to creat a dragon-tongue shape). If using an existing nail, you may want to do this on site so that you can check the height of the nail and adjust the length of your ribbon appropriately.

If nails are not allowed at your venue, forgo the ribbon and position the sign directly on the door using removable adhesive foam mounting squares, or double-sided tape. Or get two over-the-door hooks and hang the bows from them (you may need a longer piece of ribbon).

VARIATIONS

- **Retro Homespun:** Use fabric in retro-print in lieu of patterned papers. You can also use other types of silhouettes to signify girls versus boys: a hen and a rooster, a cow and a bull, and so forth.

- **Girly Romantic:** Use pale pink, gold, or sea foam papers.

ROSETTE BOUTONNIERES

LEVEL
Easy

CATEGORY
Attire

TIME
1 to 2 hours

WHEN TO START
2 to 3 weeks
before the wedding

**GROUP OR
INDIVIDUAL**
Individual

BUDGET
$10 to $20

These simple ribbon rosettes make elegant, graphic boutonnieres for your groomsmen. They can also be used to decorate napkin rings, headbands, shoes, or a simplified version of the Layered Cockade Ring Pillow (page 183).

MATERIALS
Makes 3 boutonnieres
- ¼ yard crinoline (available at Judith M. Millinery Supply, www.judithm.com)
- ½ yard 1- to 2-inch grosgrain or taffeta ribbon
- Matching thread
- 3 decorative buttons with shanks
- 3 pin backings

TOOLS
- Scissors
- Ruler, or tape measure
- Awl
- Sewing needle
- Hot glue gun and glue sticks (optional)

HOW TO

1. Make your crinoline.

For each rosette, cut a crinoline square that measures 3 × 3 inches. Make a hole roughly in the center with an awl.

2. Make your rosettes.

For each rosette, cut a length of ribbon; the chart on page 180 indicates the correct lengths for various rosette diameters. Cut straight across the ribbon, with the grain (if using grosgrain). Thread your needle and tie a knot. Fold the ribbon in half, wrong side out and match the two cut ends. Sew the cut ends together with a seam, ⅛ inch from the edge, to form a loop *(figure 1, page 180)*. Turn the ribbon inside out so the seam is inside the loop. Sew a running stitch (see page 35) along the long edge of the ribbon, beginning and ending at the seam. When you reach the end, pull the thread taut to gather the ribbon into a rosette *(figure 2, page 180)*.

Rosette radius	Ribbon length
1 inch	7 1/2 inches
1 1/4 inches	9 1/4 inches
1 1/2 inches	10 3/4 inches
1 3/4 inches	12 1/2 inches
2 inches	14 inches

figure 1

figure 2

figure 3

figure 4

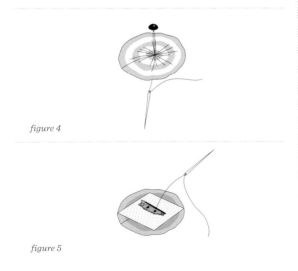

figure 5

3. Attach your rosette to your crinoline.

Thread your needle and tie a knot. Center the hole in your rosette over the hole in your crinoline. Sewing through the back toward the front, but not sewing all the way through to the top of the ribbon on the front side, make a series of 1/4-inch running stitches in a circle approximately 1/4 inch from the center, catching a few threads at the edge of each fold to secure it in place. At the last fold, tie off the thread and trim *(figure 3)*. Repeat to attach crinoline to the other two rosettes.

4. Add the button and pin backing.

Thread your needle and tie a knot. Insert the back of a button into the hole at the center of your rosette (if your button does not have a shank, center it over the hole). Sew the button to the crinoline, starting back to front *(figure 4)*. End on the back side and tie a knot. Trim your crinoline so that the edges do not peek out from behind the rosette, being careful not to cut any of your stitches as you go.

If the pin backing has holes that can be used to sew it down, sew it to your crinoline *(figure 5)*. Or squeeze hot glue onto your pin backing, press it into your crinoline, and let dry. Repeat to add a button and pin backing to the other two rosettes.

ALTERNATIVE

In lieu of ribbon, you can also make the rosettes out of 1- to 2-inch bias strips cut from taffeta or another crisp, woven fabric. To cut bias strips:

— Start with a square piece of fabric, at least 24 × 24 inches.
— Take the top left corner of the fabric and fold on the diagonal to meet the bottom right corner, making a triangle.
— Take the top right corner of your triangle and fold it to meet the bottom left corner, making a second triangle that is half the size of the first.
— Fold the bottom left corner of the fabric up along the centerline to meet the top point of the triangle.

— Using a rotary cutter and ruler, trim off the top left folded edge that you created with the last fold, cutting through all layers about $1/8$ inch from the edge.

— Decide how wide you want your bias strips to be. Holding your ruler parallel to the trimmed edge, measure and mark your strips.

— Trim your strips carefully using a rotary cutter and ruler.

— To sew two bias strips together, line the ends up with the points facing in opposite directions. Using a sewing machine or needle and thread, sew a running stitch $1/2$ inch from the edge. Iron flat along the seam.

Vary the edge treatments: straight cut, ruffled, pinked, and so forth. Layer different widths of ribbon. Try layering sheer fabrics, like tulle and organza, with opaques. To ruffle bias strips, scrape one edge of the strip between your finger and thumbnail to "unzip" the fibers into a furry fringe.

VARIATIONS

• **Retro Homespun:** In lieu of ribbon, use strips of homespun fabric. If you don't have time to hem the edges of the fabric to keep them from fraying, apply Dritz Fray Check.

• **Girly Romantic:** Using different widths of pale sheer ribbon, make larger and smaller rosettes. Layer them to create a ruffled effect.

• **Happy Graphic:** Make your rosettes out of strips of colored felt. Add a button in a bright, contrasting color.

LAYERED COCKADE RING PILLOW

with Tricia Roush,
House of Nines Design

5

LEVEL
Advanced

CATEGORY
Ceremony

TIME
6 to 8 hours

WHEN TO START
3 to 4 weeks before
the wedding

**GROUP OR
INDIVIDUAL**
Individual

BUDGET
$100 to $150
(excluding Mega Pleater)

This project requires patience and skill to master, but the results are well worth it. Grosgrain ribbon makes a lovely structured cockade layered with pleats to create a decorative ring pillow top. Use the same technique to create boutonnieres or corsages or embellishments for hats, hairpins, headbands, or purses for your bridal party.

MATERIALS

Makes 1 ring pillow

For the cockade:
- 1/4 yard crinoline (available at Judith M. Millinery Supply, www.judithm.com)
- 1 1/2 yards 2-inch grosgrain ribbon for the star
- 11-×-17-inch piece of corrugated cardboard or foam core
- One 8 1/2-×-11-inch sheet cardboard or card stock
- 1 1/4 yards 1 1/4- to 1 1/2-inch grosgrain ribbon for the outer pleated ring
- 1 1/4 yards 1-inch grosgrain ribbon for the inner pleated ring
- Matching thread
- Dritz Fray Check (or something similar, available at Jo-Ann Fabrics, at www.joann.com; optional)

For the ring pillow:
- 1/4 yard interlining fabric—medium-weight cotton or linen
- 1/4 yard cotton fabric to match the cockade for the ring pillow case

- 1 bag Poly-Fil
- Button
- 1 yard 1/8-inch ribbon
- Matching thread

TOOLS
- Sharpie
- Ruler
- Scissors
- Awl
- Straight pins
- A long, sharp, narrow needle, such as a darner needle
- Chalk pencils (such as Stabilo CarbOthello, in blue or yellow)
- Circle drafting template, with circles 3 to 4 inches in diameter
- Mega Pleater (from www.clotilde.com) and 4 or 5 (or more) old credit cards (optional)
- Craft knife
- Cutting mat
- Sewing machine
- Sewing needle
- Iron and ironing board
- Point turner (optional)
- Press cloth or dish towel

Note: These instructions make a finished cockade that measures 6 1/2 × 6 1/2 inches. You can scale the cockade up or down by using wider or narrower ribbon. Here are formulas for figuring out how much ribbon you need if you want to change the cockade size.

For the star: the measurement of the width of the ribbon, X, × 2 × 13 (where 13 = the number of pleats in the star, plus 1), then round up to the nearest quarter yard. For example, if you're using 2-inch ribbon, you would need 2 × 2 × 13 = 52 inches, so buy 54 inches or 1 1/2 yards.

For each pleated ring: the circumference of the inner edge of the ring, X, × 3, then round up to the nearest quarter yard. For example, if you want to make a ring with a 15-inch circumference, you would need 15 × 3 = 45, so buy 45 inches or 1 1/4 yards.

Tip: If your ribbon is wrinkled, turn your iron on to medium-high and lay it over the end of your ribbon. Pull the ribbon through under the iron to flatten.

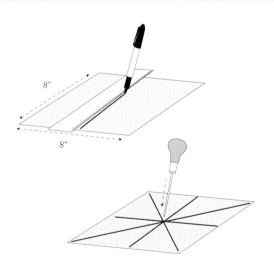

figure 1

Step 1: Prepare your crinoline backing.
1. Cut out your backing.

Using a Sharpie and a ruler, mark and cut out an 8-×-8-inch piece of crinoline (or a square 1 1/2 to 2 inches larger than your desired finished cockade size).

2. Mark it up.

Using a Sharpie and a ruler, measure and mark your square into four quadrants. Then, draw a straight diagonal line between each of the opposite corners (*figure 1*).

3. Make the center hole.

Push the awl through the center, where the lines intersect. This will help you place the cockade and will make it easier to sew a button to the center later on.

Step 2. Make the center star.
1. Measure your ribbon width.

To create the star pattern for the center of the cockade, you need to mark out 13 segments on your 2 inch grosgrain ribbon; each segment should be twice the width of the ribbon. Since ribbons are not always standard widths, use the following technique to get an accurate measurement. Lay your ribbon on your foam core or cardboard and push a pin into the board on either side of the ribbon. Remove the ribbon and lay it to the left of your two pins. Insert another pin to the left of the ribbon. You should end up with a straight row of 3 pins, which measure twice the width of the ribbon (*figure 2*).

2. Mark the ribbon for the star.

Cut the end of your ribbon straight along a ridge in the grosgrain. Lay the ribbon horizontally on your board so that the cut end aligns with the leftmost pin. If your ribbon has a selvedge (a rougher and less attractive edge), make sure it is butting against the ribbon; you will be marking this edge.

Using your pins as a guide, mark the edge of your ribbon with your chalk pencil every two ribbon widths, for a total of 13 segments *(figure 3)*. Count to make sure you have the right number of segments, then cut the ribbon straight along a ridge in the grosgrain at the end of the last segment.

3. Create the folds.

Thread your needle and tie a knot in one end, leaving the other end loose (do not knot both ends of the thread). Hold the end of the marked ribbon in your left hand, with the marks facing right *(figure 4a)*. Take the end of the ribbon and fold it under so the cut end meets the first mark *(figure 4b)*. Then, fold the ribbon under again, so that the end is tucked squarely between two layers of ribbon *(figure 4c)*. Bring your needle up through the bottom right corner of the folded ribbon (the corner where the cut end is nested). Make 2 whip stitches (see page 43) through the corner, catching all 3 layers of ribbon, to secure the cut end in place *(figure 4d)*.

Without cutting your thread, let go of the stitched folds and let them fall loose and rest under your length of ribbon, which extends away from you. Pinch the ribbon into a fold at the second mark in your ribbon *(figure 5a, page 186)*. Pierce your needle through the top right corner of this fold, about 1/8 inch from the edge *(figure 5b, page 186)*. Keep the fold on the needle; do not pull it all the way through. Keeping the fold you have just created on your needle, pinch the ribbon again at the next mark and pierce your needle through the top right corner of the next fold *(figure 5c, page 186)*. Again, do not pull the needle through; keep the folds on the needle. Continue folding and piercing, loading up your needle with even folds *(figure 5d, page 186)*.

When you get to the end of the ribbon, make your last fold and pierce your needle through the bottom corner of the cut end (it should meet up neatly

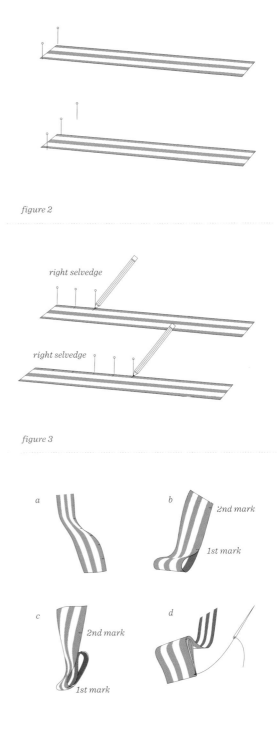

figure 2

right selvedge

right selvedge

figure 3

a

b

2nd mark

1st mark

c

2nd mark

1st mark

d

figure 4

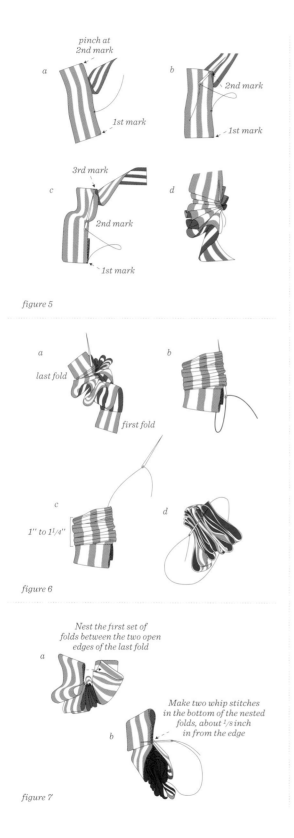

figure 5

figure 6

Nest the first set of
folds between the two open
edges of the last fold

Make two whip stitches
in the bottom of the nested
folds, about ⅛ inch
in from the edge

figure 7

with the rest of your folds) *(figure 6a)*. With your needle still pierced through all your folds, align the folds so that they make a neat stack *(figure 6b)*. You should be able to pinch the stack between your left thumb and forefinger with the needle pointing straight away from you on the right-hand side, holding all the folds in place. Now, pull the needle all the way through *(figure 6c)*, keeping the tension loose. Once the needle is pulled through, hold the folds in your left hand with the sewn edge on the inside. The folds should be loose enough so that, taken together, they measure about 1 to 1¼ inches across. You want the folds to be loose and springy—not pulled too tight—so that you have room to spread them out later into a star shape.

Now, pierce your needle through the last fold and the cut end *(figure 6d)*. This will pin the last cut end down to the last fold, securing it (similar to the way in which you secured the first cut end at one corner). Make two whip stitches along the edge (similar to the first cut end), pull tight, tie a knot, and cut your thread.

4. Nest and tack the folds to form a continuous ring.

Tie a new knot in your thread. Hold the first set of folds in your left hand, and the last set of folds in your right. Nest the first set of folds between the two open edges of the last fold. This will connect the two ends in a clean fashion so that they make a continuous ring *(figure 7a)*. Nudge the nested folds into place so that they are as closely aligned as possible. Hold the nested folds in between your thumb and middle finger in your left hand, grasping the rest of the folds in your palm. Make two whip stitches in the bottom right corner of the nested folds, about ⅛ inch from the edge *(figure 7b)*. Pull tight, tie a knot, and cut your thread.

Holding the nested fold toward you, fold the bottom left corner up and under to form a triangle shape *(figure 8a)*. Make two straight stitches through the triangle, parallel to the hypotenuse, to tack it into place *(figure 8b)*. Tie a knot and cut your thread.

5. Pin the star down.

Holding your folds in both hands, begin spreading them out so that they are evenly spaced and all facing the same direction to create overlapping diagonal folds that make a radiating star shape *(figure 9a)*. Center your folds on your crinoline and continue to adjust the folds until they are evenly spaced, using the lines on the crinoline to guide their placement. Once you are happy with their position, pin the folds down. Pin one fold, then pin the fold on the opposite side. Continue until all the folds are pinned down *(figure 9b)*. If the crinoline buckles, you may be pulling too tight as you pin down opposite sides; unpin, loosen, and re-pin.

6. Stitch the center of the star.

Thread a sewing needle and tie a knot. Starting with the nested fold, adjust the inner folds of the star so that they make a smooth, continuous ring. Push your needle up through the first fold, about 1/8 inch from the inner corner. Pull taut and sew a short stitch into the fold. Repeat for each fold, adjusting the position of the folds as you go.

7. Tack down the folds.

Hold the star with the crinoline side facing you *(figure 10)*. The crinoline should be transparent enough that you can see the edge of each fold through it. Make a series of 1/4-inch running stitches in a circle approximately 1/2 inch from the center, catching the back of each fold to secure it. Do not sew through the front of the folds. At the last fold, tie off the thread and trim.

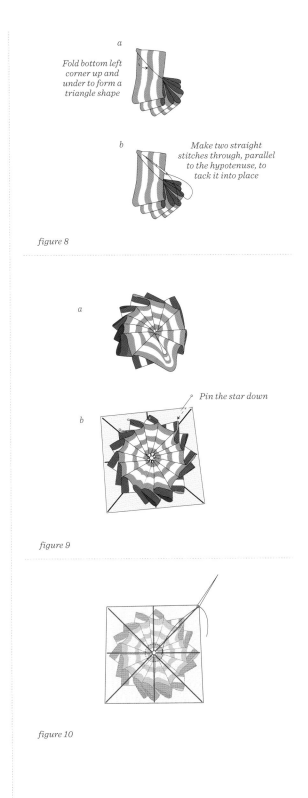

a

Fold bottom left corner up and under to form a triangle shape

b

Make two straight stitches through, parallel to the hypotenuse, to tack it into place

figure 8

a

Pin the star down

b

figure 9

figure 10

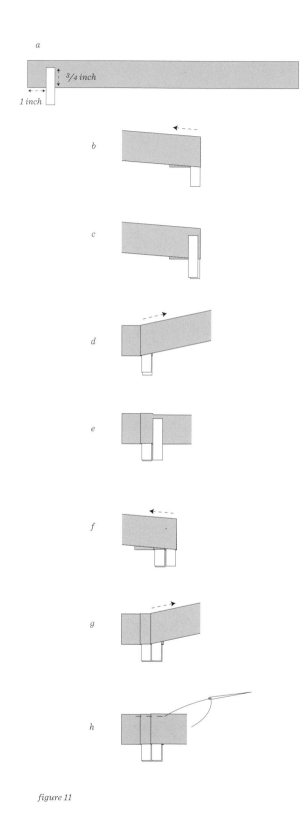

figure 11

Step 3: Pleat the ribbon for the inner and outer rings.

This project calls for an outer ring of knife pleats, and an inner ring of box pleats. You are going to pleat two lengths of ribbon, each about 15 inches long, into rings, and then layer them so that the knife pleats peek out from behind the box pleats. To simplify, you can use just one type of pleat for both rings. To change the size of the rings, simply pleat more or less ribbon, and adjust the circle template size to match their desired position.

1. Mark the crinoline.

Center a 4 1/4-inch circle template onto the back of your crinoline, and trace the circle with a Sharpie. This circle will mark the inner edge of your rings.

2. Make the knife pleats for the outer ring.

For one knife-pleated ring, you'll need to make a strip of pleated ribbon that is at least 15 inches long when pleated.

Pleat by Hand:

Using a craft knife, ruler, and cutting mat, cut four rectangles, or gauges, out of your card stock. The gauges should be 1/4 inch wide and as long as your ribbon is wide.

Lay your 1 1/4- to 1 1/2-inch ribbon, right-side up, on your work surface. If one edge of your ribbon looks rougher, place that side facing up. Lay your first gauge perpendicular to your ribbon, about 1 inch from the left end, so it covers the bottom 3/4 inch of your ribbon (*figure 11a*). Fold the long end of the ribbon over the gauge, from right to left (*figure 11b*). Place a second gauge on top of the first (*figure 11c*). There will be one layer of ribbon between the gauges. Fold the ribbon back over the second gauge, from left to right (*figure 11d*). This forms the first pleat. Lay your third gauge on top of your ribbon, this time placing it adjacent and to the right of your first two gauges (*figure 11e*). Fold the ribbon over the gauge, from right to left (*figure 11f*). Place your fourth gauge on top of the third gauge and fold the ribbon, from left to right, over the fourth gauge (*figure 11g*). This forms the second pleat.

Thread a sewing needle and make a knot at one end. Leaving the gauges in place, secure the pleats using a 1/3-inch running stitch (see page 35) along the top edge (*figure 11h*). Leave the needle and thread in the ribbon (do not tie a knot and cut). Remove the gauges from the first two pleats and use them to make the next two pleats. Stitch in place and repeat until your pleated ribbon measures at least 15 inches long. Trim the ribbon, leaving about 1 inch extra at each end.

Lay a press cloth or dish towel over the pleated ribbon with the pleats facing toward you. Press gently with your iron on the steam setting. Iron toward you to make sure the ribbon does not catch. Leave in place until cool and dry. Leave the thread in the ribbon.

Or Using a Pleater:

Note: the Mega Pleater makes one strip of knife-pleated ribbon up to 22 inches long.

Lay your pleater on your ironing board, folds facing away from you. Lay your 1 1/4- to 1 1/2-inch ribbon over the folds in the pleater, with the cut end hanging over the edge by about 1 inch. Lift the second fold in the pleater (the first one will be too shallow to use) and push your ribbon into it using a credit card to create a crisp pleat (*figure 12*). Repeat with each fold, leaving the cards in place. When you run out of cards, gently remove the cards from the first pleats and use them to make the next set of pleats. Use the cards to gently nudge and straighten your row of pleats as you go. Continue until your entire length of ribbon is pleated. Gently remove all cards.

With the ribbon still in the pleater, lay a press cloth or dish towel over the ribbon. Press gently with your iron on the steam setting. Iron toward you to

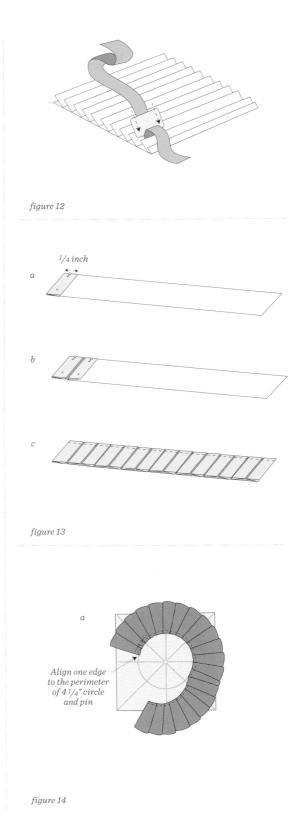

figure 12

1/4 inch

a

b

c

figure 13

a

Align one edge to the perimeter of 4 1/4" circle and pin

figure 14

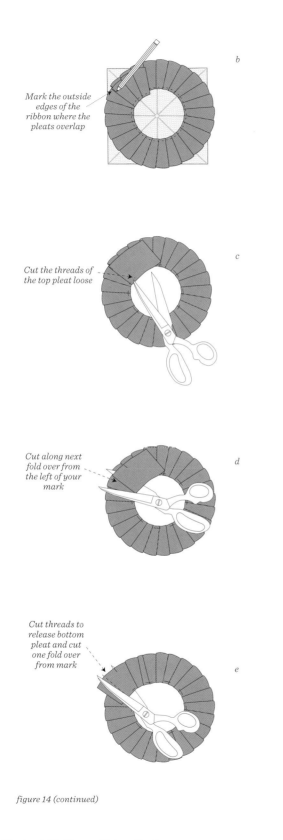

Mark the outside edges of the ribbon where the pleats overlap

b

Cut the threads of the top pleat loose

c

Cut along next fold over from the left of your mark

d

Cut threads to release bottom pleat and cut one fold over from mark

e

figure 14 (continued)

make sure the ribbon does not catch. Leave in place until cool and dry. Trim the ribbon, leaving 1 inch on either end. Once the ribbon is dry, gently roll the pleater and flex the folds to release the ribbon.

Beginning at one end with the pleats facing you and the rough edge of the ribbon closest to the needle, feed the ribbon through your sewing machine and sew using a straight stitch about 1/8 inch from the edge. Sew one 2- to 3-inch section at a time, straightening the pleats in each section with both hands to ensure they are evenly spaced. Make sure you are catching all the layers.

3. Make the box pleats for the inner ring.

Hold your 1-inch grosgrain ribbon so that the nicer side (if there is one) is facing up and the end is in your right hand. Fold into a box pleat: fold the ribbon toward you, then fold it away, so that the resulting fold is 1/4 inch wide and is shaped like an S. Pin the pleat in place, with the pin running parallel to the grain of the ribbon *(figure 13a, page 189)*. If one selvedge of the ribbon is rougher than the other, insert the pins so that their heads are toward the rougher side; this is also the side you will stitch the pleats down on. Skip about 1/2 inch of ribbon and fold it away from you to meet the fold you just made. Then fold back in the opposite direction; this time the fold will be shaped like a Z. Pin into place *(figure 13b, page 189)*. Skip 1/2 inch of ribbon and repeat, butting each fold up against the next. Continue until the pleated ribbon measures at least 15 inches. Using a sewing machine, sew the pleats into place using a running stitch and matching thread, about 1/8 inch from the edge *(figure 13c, page 189)*. Remove the pins as you go. Once you have sewn the entire length, lay the ribbon on your ironing board and hold your iron over it (without pressing onto the ribbon itself), and blast it with steam. The steam will fluff up the pleats and remove any holes left over from the removed pins.

Step 4: Finish your cockade.

1. Connect the outer ring (knife pleat).

Lay the crinoline on your work surface, back side up. Align one edge to the perimeter of your 4¹⁄₄-inch circle and pin down *(figure 14a, page 189)*. Walk the pleats around the circle and, when the ring is complete, align the last pleat to cover the first pleat. Mark the outside edges of the ribbon where the pleats overlap *(figure 14b)*. Cut the threads of the top pleat loose *(figure 14c)*. Cut along the next fold over to the left of your mark, in the "valley" of the pleat *(figure 14d)*. Unpin the bottom pleat, and cut the thread to release it. Cut along the next fold over to the left of your mark, in the "valley" of the pleat *(figure 14e)*. Align the two cut ends, and sew them together using a straight stitch *(figure 14f)*. Fold the pleat back down at the remaining mark. The two cut ends should tuck neatly behind it, allowing the pleats to form a continuous ring.

2. Connect the inner ring (box pleat).

Repeat the process, connecting the two ends of your strip of box pleats into a continuous ring. You will now have two rings of pleats *(figure 15)*.

3. Join the two outer rings.

Lay the box-pleated ring on top of the knife-pleated ring, and rotate them so that the sewn seams of each ring are aligned. Sew them together in a running stitch, as close to the inner edge as you can while catching both rings *(figure 16)*. From here on out, treat them as one piece.

4. Assemble your cockade.

Slip the ring of pleats over the star, like a collar, snuggling it in place so that the pleats peek out. Rotate it so that the sewn seams of the rings and star are aligned. Flip the cockade over to confirm that the inside of the ring is aligned with the 4¹⁄₄-inch circle. Sewing from the backside, sew the ring into place along the inner edge with matching thread using a running stitch *(figure 17, page 192)*.

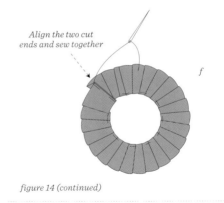

Align the two cut ends and sew together

f

figure 14 (continued)

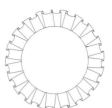

Box pleats

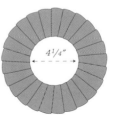

4¹⁄₄"

Knife pleats

figure 15

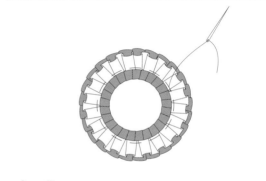

figure 16

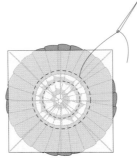

figure 17

5. Attach a button and ribbon.

Fold your ¹/₂-yard length of ¹/₄-inch ribbon in half and push the folded end through the hole in the center of the crinoline. Push the back of the button through the hole. Thread a straight pin through the back of the crinoline on one side of the button, through the button hole and the ribbon fold, and through the crinoline on the other side of the button. This will hold the button and ribbon securely in place. Make sure that the sharp end of the pin does not pierce through the front of the cockade.

Trim the crinoline around the edge of your outermost ring of stitches, leaving about a ¹/₄-inch border that will be used to sew the cockade onto the ring pillow.

Step 5: Make the ring pillow.

Follow the instructions on pages 47 to 49 for making a ring pillow. Make sure the pillow is large enough so that your cockade fits comfortably on top of it. When you have completed your ring pillow, center the cockade on it, and sew around the crinoline edge using a running stitch until the cockade is secure.

VARIATIONS

• **Girly Romantic:** Choose grosgrain or moiré ribbon in pale pink, sea foam, or gold—or a combination of all three.

• **Happy Graphic:** Make your cockades using colorful stripes and solids, such as reds or yellows.

• **Organic Minimal:** Use linen ribbon in a variety of neutral shades, or use heavy-weight fabric strips to make your cockades.

RIBBON DRINK FLAGS

6

LEVEL
Easy

....

CATEGORY
Reception

....

TIME
3 to 4 hours

....

WHEN TO START
2 to 3 weeks
before the wedding

....

**GROUP OR
INDIVIDUAL**
Group

· · ·

· *Station 1: Trim the ribbon.*
· *Station 2: Trim the dowels.*
· *Station 3: Tie and glue the ribbon.*
· *Station 4: Cut dragon tongues
  in the ribbon ends.*

....

BUDGET
$40 to $50

With just a few inexpensive wooden dowels and a few yards of ribbon, you can create beautiful and festive stir sticks for your cocktail hour. Be sure to test a few types of ribbon before purchasing in bulk, as some ribbons hold their shape better than others.

MATERIALS

Makes 100 drink flags
- 22 yards $3/8$-inch ribbon in a variety of colors and patterns, such as grosgrain, satin, or gingham
- Twenty-five 36-inch wooden dowels ($1/4$-inch diameter)

TOOLS
- Garden shears
- Ruler
- Scissors
- Hot glue gun and glue sticks

HOW TO

1. Trim your dowels and ribbon.

Using garden shears, trim your dowels into 8-inch lengths (each dowel yields four drink stirrers). Cut your ribbon into 7- to 8-inch lengths.

2. Tie your knots.

For each drink flag, fold a length of ribbon in half. Center the dowel over the folded ribbon, with the top of the dowel about $1/2$ inch over the top edge of the ribbon. Holding the dowel in place with your right hand, open the loop in the fold with your left hand and thread the two ends of the ribbon through the loop *(figure 1, page 195)*. Pull the knot tight around the dowel. Slide the ribbon down the dowel and apply a dab of hot glue to the spot where the center of the flag will go, about $1/2$ inch from the top of the dowel. Slide the ribbon up over the hot glue, pull the knot tight, and hold it in place for a few seconds, until dry.

3. Trim the ribbon ends.

Fold the ribbon end in half, and cut toward the fold at a 45-degree angle to create a dragon-tongue shape *(figure 2)*.

VARIATIONS

You can adapt these drink flags to a variety of aesthetics simply through your choice of ribbon.

- **Retro Homespun:** Choose colorful striped or checked ribbons, mixed with coordinating solids.

- **Organic Minimal:** Use neutral stitched ribbons, linen ribbon, or strips of frayed fabric.

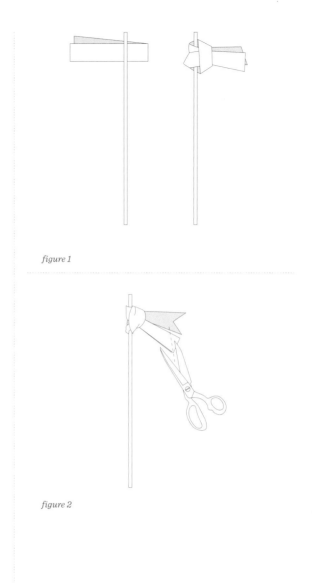

figure 1

figure 2

BOW-TIE NAPKINS

Arranged in a bow tie shape, a simple folded napkin and book-cloth-covered toilet paper tube segment become an elegant addition to your table setting. Although other fabrics can work as well, book cloth is the easiest to wrap, crease, and fold neatly, and it is available in a range of colors from some local art supply stores and bookbinders, as well as online bookbinding supply shops (see "Resources," page 249). Because these are best assembled on the day of your wedding, make the napkin rings ahead of time and then ask your caterer to make the bows using rented napkins.

LEVEL
Easy

CATEGORY
Reception

TIME
2 to 3 hours

WHEN TO START
3 to 4 weeks before
the wedding

**GROUP OR
INDIVIDUAL**
Group

· · ·

· *Station 1: Cut toilet paper tubes.*
· *Station 2: Cut book cloth.*
· *Station 3: Wrap tubes with
book cloth.*

BUDGET
$25 to $50
(excluding napkins)

MATERIALS
Makes 100 napkin rings
· 35 toilet paper tubes
· Six 21-×-24-inch sheets
book cloth

TOOLS
· Craft knife
· Ruler
· Pencil
· Cutting mat
· Rubber cement, or clear-drying
craft glue
· Bone folder (optional)

HOW TO:
1. Cut your toilet paper tubes and book cloth.
Cut your toilet paper tubes crosswise into 1 1/2-inch segments using a craft knife, keeping the shape intact; each tube should yield three rings. To create even edges around your rings, measure 1 1/2 inches from the edge and mark with a pencil; rotate your tube 1/4 inch and measure and mark again. Repeat until you have a series of marks around the circumference of your tube, and cut along these marks *(figure 1, page 198)*.

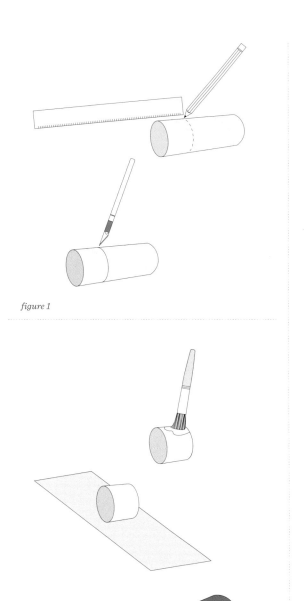

figure 1

figure 2

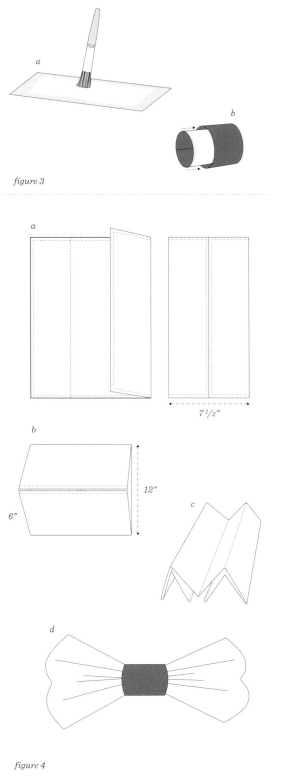

figure 3

a

7 1/2"

b

12"

6"

c

d

figure 4

Using a craft knife, ruler, and cutting mat, trim the book cloth into 100 rectangles each 3 inches wide and long enough to wrap around your ring completely, about 6 inches—these are for the outer covering. Then, cut one hundred 5 1/4-×-1-inch pieces—these strips are to finish the inside edge.

2. Wrap your tubes.

For all tubes, lay one of the large book cloth rectangles, right-side down, on your work surface, long side facing you. Dab glue on a toilet paper ring. Center the ring on the book cloth, and, starting at one end, roll the book cloth tightly around the tube and secure using a dab of glue. Spread a thin layer of glue inside the overhanging book cloth on one end of the tube. Gently fold the book cloth inside the tube, pressing with your fingers or a bone folder as you go to get a smooth edge and tucking as necessary. Repeat with the book cloth on the other end *(figure 2)*.

Now, apply a thin layer of adhesive to the back side of one of the smaller book cloth strips, except for the first and last 1 inch on either end *(figure 3a)*. Roll it into a small tube a little smaller than the cardboard tube, with the right-side of the book cloth facing in. Slip the small tube inside the cardboard tube *(figure 3b)*, center it, and press it in place to cover the center 1 inch of the interior of the tube, making sure to expand the roll as you do so to fit the shape of the tube. When you have it nicely placed, gently pull the first and last edges back, and put a dab of adhesive underneath to secure them. Repeat with the rest of the tubes.

3. Assemble your napkins.

Lay a napkin flat on your work surface. Fold the left and right edges of the napkin in to meet at the vertical center line *(figure 4a)*. Accordion fold the napkin into four segments *(figure 4b)*, then flip the napkin fold-side down while holding the folds in place. Release the napkin; it will make

an M shape *(figure 4c)*. Thread the folded napkin through the ring. Shape the ends to make a flared bow *(figure 4d)*.

VARIATIONS

• **Retro Homespun:** Cover your napkin rings in patterned fabric. Or wrap them in yarn or ribbon. Unroll some of the yarn from the skein and wind it into a smaller, long skein that fits through the opening of your ring. Hot glue one end of the yarn to the inside of your tube, or wind it around the side wall of the tube once and tie a small knot. Wind the yarn around and around the side wall of the tube, working your way around the tube, and pushing the yarn closer together as you wind so the cardboard does not show through. Go around twice if you need to. When the tube is covered, trim the yarn, and tuck the end securely under some of the previously wound yarn on the inside of the tube so the loose end doesn't show. Secure the end with glue, if desired.

• **Girly Romantic:** Cover your napkin rings in gold or pink moiré book cloth. Use napkins in complementary colors.

PUNCHED-PAPER FLOWER CENTERPIECE

8

LEVEL
Easy

. . . .

CATEGORY
Reception

. . . .

TIME
3 to 4 hours

. . . .

WHEN TO START
2 to 3 weeks
before the wedding

. . . .

**GROUP OR
INDIVIDUAL**
Group
. . .

• *Station 1: Punch the flowers.*
• *Station 2: Fold the flowers.*
• *Station 3: Insert the floral pips
and assemble the flowers.*
• *Station 4: Attach the flowers
to the branches.*

. . . .

BUDGET
$40 to $50

Pretty papers, punched into flower shapes and attached to simple branches, make a striking floral display. Make multiples and use them to accent a welcome or guest-book table or to create dramatic, sculptural centerpieces at your reception. If transportation to the venue is a concern, the flowers can be made in advance and then attached to the branches the day before or the morning of the wedding.

MATERIALS
Makes 1 centerpiece
• Five to ten 11-×-17-inch sheets
patterned paper
• 1 to 2 bundles of floral pips
• Three 48-inch bleached
Japanese Mitsumata branches

TOOLS
• Large and small flower punches
• Sewing needle
• Hot glue gun and glue sticks
• Glue dots or double-sided tape

HOW TO

1. Make the flowers.

Punch large and small flowers out of your patterned papers. For each flower, place the flower, right-side up, on your work surface and gently fold and unfold it along each axis to give the flower dimension *(figure 1, page 202)*. Pierce the center of a large and small flower with your needle to make a small hole. Thread two or three floral pips through the hole in your small flower, then through the hole in your large flower. Push the flowers toward the pips until you are satisfied with their placement. Fold the pip stems down and secure them with a bead of hot glue *(figure 2, page 202)*. Repeat to make all the flowers.

figure 1

2. Decorate the branches.

Place a glue dot or small piece of double-sided tape on the back of each flower and attach them to the branches, repositioning them until you are happy with your composition. To permanently adhere each flower, squeeze a bead of hot glue onto the back of a flower and attach it to the branch, holding it in place until it dries.

VARIATIONS

• **Girly Romantic:** Punch flowers out of several shades of tissue paper for a more ethereal look.

• **Found:** Punch flowers out of a variety of found papers in a similar color palette (to create a more natural flower look), such as security envelopes or newspaper.

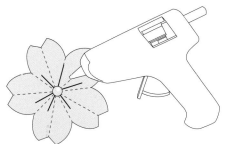

figure 2

CREPE PAPER–FLOWER CAKE TOPPER

9

Crepe paper flowers are beautiful, versatile, and easy to make. This cake topper uses four to six large anemones, paired with a striped ribbon base, to create an elegant, graphic look. Crepe paper flowers are also wonderful for bouquets, boutonnieres, or aisle markers (twist the stems together to make a garland).

LEVEL
Moderate

CATEGORY
Reception

TIME
3 to 4 hours

WHEN TO START
2 to 3 weeks before
the wedding

**GROUP OR
INDIVIDUAL**
Individual

BUDGET
$25 to $50

MATERIALS
Makes 1 cake topper

- 4 pieces 18-inch paper-covered floral wire
- 1 roll white crepe paper, about 10 × 49 inches
- Green floral tape, or 1/4 roll green crepe paper, about 10 × 18 inches
- 1/4 roll black crepe paper, about 10 × 18 inches
- 1/4 yard white cotton fabric
- One 6-×-1-inch Styrofoam disc (available at craft and floral supply shops)
- 1 yard 1-inch grosgrain ribbon (optional)

TOOLS

- Anemone Petal template (available online at www .chroniclebooks.com/ handmade-weddings)
- Scissors
- Small brush
- Craft glue
- Iron and ironing board
- Rotary cutter
- Ruler
- Cutting mat
- Straight pins
- Support that is taller and narrower than your disc, such as a soda can
- Hot glue gun and glue sticks

HOW TO

1. Make the flower stamens.

This design calls for four to six large anemones. For each flower, start by making the stamen. Cut a 12-inch length of floral wire. Using scissors, cut out a 4-×-4-inch square of white crepe paper. Wad it into a ball, about 1/2 inch in diameter. Cut out a 2-×-2-inch square of white crepe paper, and brush a light layer of craft glue

over one side, covering the entire surface. Press the ball onto the end of your floral wire so that the wire punctures the wad but does not pierce all the way through. Center the crepe paper square over the wad, glue-side down, and fold over it, twisting the paper's ends around the stem to create a buttonlike stamen *(figure 1)*. Repeat for all of your flowers.

Wrap the stems with floral tape. Or cut a 1/2-×-4-inch rectangle of green crepe paper, with the long side running across the grain (the creases in the crepe paper form the grain; cut across them, in the same direction that the crepe paper stretches). Hold this rectangle wrong-side up, and brush craft glue onto one short end. Starting at the base of the button, wrap the paper tightly around the stem, working your way down the stem until the twisted white crepe paper is completely covered *(figure 2)*. When you reach the end, brush craft glue onto the end of the green crepe paper, and twist around the stem to secure it. Wrap the remaining stems.

Cut a 1-×-5-inch rectangle of black crepe paper with the long side running across the grain. Using your scissors, make 3/4-inch-deep cuts in one long side, about 1/8 inch wide *(figure 3)*. The fringes will overlap, so don't worry about making them perfect. Brush craft glue along the wrong side of the unfringed edge and, starting at the base of the button, roll it tightly, creating a layered sunburst around the button *(figure 4)*. Repeat for the remaining flowers.

2. Make the petals.

For each flower, cut out 12 white petals, each about 1 1/2 × 2 inches, roughly following the Anemone Petal template. Cut the petals so that the width of the petal runs across the grain. The petals should stretch and widen when gently pulled in opposite directions. For efficiency, accordion-fold your crepe paper with the grain into 2-inch sections, three or four times, and cut out several petals at once. For each petal, shape it by sculpting the crepe paper. First, pinch the petal between your

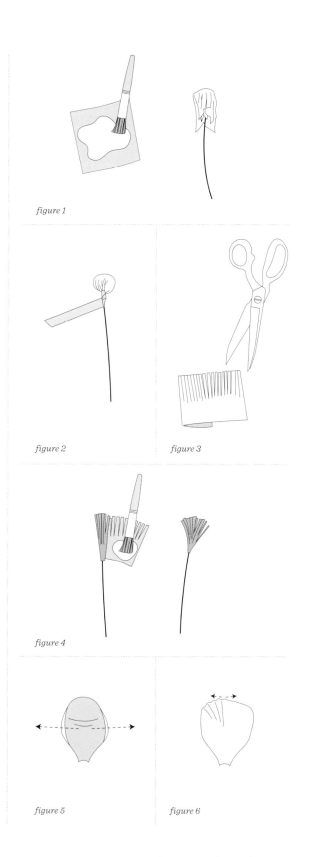

figure 1

figure 2

figure 3

figure 4

figure 5

figure 6

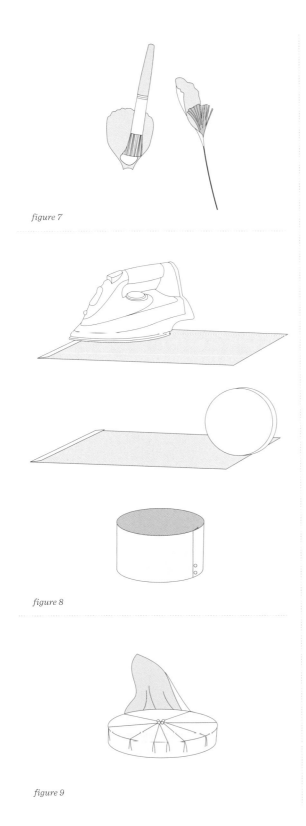

figure 7

figure 8

figure 9

thumbs and forefingers, holding it on the left and right sides with your thumbs pressed into the center of the petal and your forefingers supporting the petal from behind. Push gently away from you with your thumbs, creating a gently cupped shape *(figure 5, page 205)*. Next, ruffle the edges by pinching the edge of the petal between your thumbs and forefingers, keeping your thumbs close together, and pulling gently in opposite directions. Continue working your way around the petal in 1/2-inch segments, to create a ruffled edge *(figure 6, page 205)*.

3. Add the petals.

Brush the inside bottom end of a petal (about the bottom 1/4 inch) with craft glue. Attach the petal to your stamen, just below the button, pressing and wrapping it slightly around the stem *(figure 7)*. Continue attaching petals in a ring around the stamen, overlapping each petal with the next. Add two to three more rings of petals, positioning each ring slightly higher than the next, until you are happy with the fullness of your flower.

Wrap the base of the petals with floral tape. Or cut a 1/2-×-4-inch rectangle of green crepe paper, with the long side running across the grain. Brush one short end with glue and, starting at the base of the petals, wrap the paper tightly around the stem, working your way down the stem until the twisted bottoms of the petals are completely covered. When you reach the end, brush craft glue onto the end of the floral tape or green crepe paper, and twist around the stem to secure it.

4. Cover the base with fabric.

Iron the fabric. Using a rotary cutter, ruler, and cutting mat, cut the ironed fabric to a 7-×-20-inch rectangle. *Note: If you are using a Styrofoam disc that is not 6 × 1 inches, calculate the length and width as follows:*
- *length = (diameter × 3.14) + 1 inch, rounded up to the nearest inch; or measure the circumference with a tape measure and add 1 inch.*

- *width = diameter + height; or run your measuring tape from the top center, over the side, to the bottom center.*

Lay your fabric, right-side down, on your ironing board. Fold a 1/2-inch seam on one short end, and iron flat. Transfer your fabric to your work surface. Center your Styrofoam disc on its side on the fabric at the rough short edge and roll the fabric all the way around the disc so it meets the folded seam. Pin the folded seam over the rough edge with two to three straight pins (*figure 8*).

Place your Styrofoam disc on your support. This will keep the fabric from wrinkling as you wrap the first side of the base. Beginning at the seam, push the fabric toward the center of the disc and fold the fabric into small, overlapping pleats, each facing the same direction. Work your way around the fabric, smoothing the pleats and holding them in place at the center as you go. If needed, insert pins as you go to keep the pleats in place. When you have completed the circle, smooth the pleats down and pin them in place. Turn the disc over and repeat on the other side (*figure 9*).

5. Arrange your flowers.

Arrange your flowers on top of the base, facing out, until you are pleased with their composition. If needed, trim the stems or curl them inward to keep them from sticking out. Affix the stems to the base with hot glue. Alternatively, hold two flowers in your hand, adjusting their arrangement until you are pleased with it, and then twist the stems together to lock them in place. Add the remaining flowers, one by one. Secure the flower bouquet to your base using hot glue.

6. Decorate the base of the cake topper (optional).

If desired, you can decorate the base of the cake topper with ribbon. Cut a 20-inch length of ribbon and wrap it around the base so that the seam lines up with the seam in the fabric. Pin in place. Cut a 5 1/4-inch length of ribbon. Loop the ends together, overlapping the ends by 1/4 inch. Affix the seam with hot glue and flatten to create a 2 1/2-inch rectangle. Cut a 3-inch length of ribbon and make another loop, flattening to create a 1 1/2-inch rectangle. Apply hot glue to the seam of the 1 1/2-inch rectangle and center it over the right side of the 2 1/2-inch rectangle. Press together to form two stacked rectangles. Cut a 2 1/4-inch length of ribbon. Fold the two long edges toward the center and iron into place. Wrap the ironed ribbon around the center of your rectangles and fasten on the back side with hot glue. You now have a layered ribbon bow. Apply hot glue to the back of the bow and attach it to the side of the base, opposite the seam.

VARIATIONS

Crepe paper flowers come in all shapes and sizes, from tulips to roses to poppies. Look at photographs of your favorite flowers, and experiment with different petal shapes, stamens, and colors of crepe paper to create your desired look and feel.

- **Retro Homespun:** Make colorful California poppies, cupping the petals deeply and using four to five petals per flower. Cover the base in gingham or colorful solid fabric.

- **Girly Romantic:** Cover your cake topper with peonies. Choose very pale pink crepe paper (this can be hard to find—see "Resources," page 249), and follow the instructions for the anemone, omitting the fringe around the stamen and adding upward of forty to fifty petals. To create a full effect, start the petals lower on the stem, making each ring slightly higher than the last.

CREPE PAPER–CRACKER FAVORS

10

Modeled after English Christmas crackers, these favors are both elegant and fun. Guests hold the cracker in their right hand, cross arms, and each pull a cracker end. The cracker makes a satisfying pop as it opens. Adding a paper band inscribed with guests' names allows these crackers to double as place cards, or you can just write a word of thanks on each.

LEVEL
Moderate

CATEGORY
Favors and gifts

TIME
6 to 8 hours

WHEN TO START
2 to 3 weeks
before the wedding

**GROUP OR
INDIVIDUAL**
Group (after printing)

. . .

- *Station 1: Cover the toilet paper tubes.*
- *Station 2: Fill the tubes with favor contents.*
- *Station 3: Cut the crepe paper.*
- *Station 4: Wrap the tubes.*
- *Station 5: Tie and shape the ends.*
- *Station 6: Cut and attach the cracker band.*

BUDGET
$50 to $75
(excluding favor contents)

MATERIALS
Makes 100 favors

- Fifty 8 1/2-×-11-inch sheets decorative paper
- 100 toilet paper tubes
- 100 Christmas cracker snaps (see "Resources," page 249)
- 100 sets small party favors, such as tissue paper crowns, candies, or riddles
- 14 rolls (about 10 × 49 inches per roll) crepe paper for the outer layer
- 14 rolls (about 10 × 49 inches per roll) tissue paper for the inner layer (optional)
- 60 yards 1/8-inch seam binding tape or decorative ribbon
- Forty 8 1/2-×-11-inch sheets text-weight paper for bands

TOOLS
- Cracker Band template (available online at www .chroniclebooks.com/ handmade-weddings)
- Font: Compendium
- Paper cutter with interchangeable rotary blades
- Straight rotary blade
- Perforated rotary blade
- Glue sticks
- Clear tape
- Scissors
- Ruler
- Pencil
- Double-sided tape
- Inkjet printer, or a calligraphy pen and ink (see page 169)

HOW TO

1. Wrap your toilet paper tubes.

Using a paper cutter with the straight blade, cut one hundred 5-×-4-inch pieces of decorativepaper (cut out one test piece first to ensure that it wraps around a toilet paper tube, covering the entire surface;

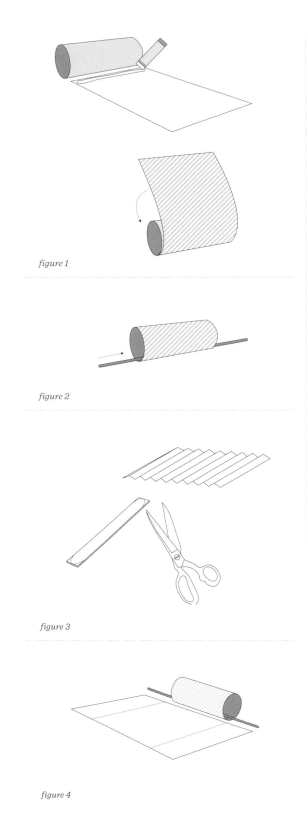

figure 1

figure 2

figure 3

figure 4

the measurements here assume a 1 1/2-×-4-inch toilet paper tube). For each toilet paper tube, apply glue along the short ends of the decorative paper with a glue stick, and then wrap the tube (*figure 1*).

2. Insert your cracker snap and favors.

Insert a cracker snap into each tube so that the ends are poking out both sides (*figure 2*). Secure each to the inside of the tube by placing a small piece of clear tape to one side of the snapping mechanism. Insert your favors into the tube.

3. Cut your tissue and crepe paper.

Using the paper cutter witht the straight blade, cut one hundred ten 6-×-11 1/2-inch pieces of crepe paper for your outer layers, and one hundred ten 6-×-13 1/2-inch pieces of tissue paper for your inner layers. The paper should be big enough to wrap completely around the tube and extend about 3 inches beyond either end of the tube. Accordion-fold the paper into 1/2-inch lengths and cut out a half-scallop with scissors (*figure 3*).

Insert the perforated blade into your paper cutter. For each piece of paper, cut two perforated lines parallel to the short ends of each piece marking the center 4 inches (or the length of your toilet paper tube). To confirm where to cut, lay your paper lengthwise on your work surface. Center your toilet paper tube on it and, using a ruler, measure the distance from each short end to the edge of the tube. These lines will allow the favor to break open easily when the ends are pulled (*figure 4*).

4. Wrap your tubes.

Wrap the inner layer of tissue paper around each tube, aligning the perforations with the ends of the tube. Secure the paper with double-sided tape. Wrap the outer layer around each tube, again aligning the perforations and securing with double-sided tape (*figure 5*). For each tube, cut two 10-inch lengths of seam binding or decorative ribbon. Tie a ribbon around the crepe paper at each end of the tube, finishing with a square knot or bow. Use scissors to trim the ends at a 45-degree angle *(figure 6)*.

5. Add your message.

Print or handwrite your guests' names or your thank-you message onto strips of plain or colored text-weight paper. To create the diagonal band shown in the photograph, use the Cracker Band template. Customize your message (or leave it blank, to handwrite later), print it on text-weight paper, and trim. Or make your own diagonal band. Cut out a 2-×-6-inch strip of paper. Spiral it around your tube and mark a straight line across the ends of the strip where they meet each other on the back side. Unravel the strip, and cut each end at the marked line. The line ends should be angled, and when the paper is wrapped around the tube, they should meet so that the angled points are side-by-side and just touching, forming a straight line *(figure 7)*. Use this as a template for cutting the rest of your strips. Attach the strips with double-sided tape.

VARIATIONS

Crackers are associated with the Christmas holidays, so they can be especially fitting at a winter wedding. That said, in the right colors, they make great favors year-round.

- **Girly Romantic:** Wrap your crackers in pale pink, sea foam, or gold crepe paper (or all three). For the best color selection, look for German crepe paper—see "Resources," page 249. If desired, add details like millinery birds to the ends of your crackers and use Nelly Script for your font.

- **Found:** Use Nelly Script for your font and wrap your crackers in kraft paper and fill with fun found trinkets and candies.

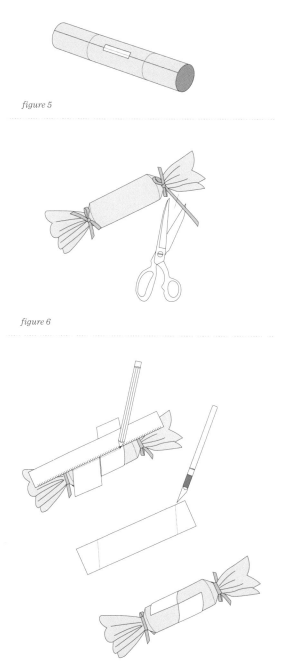

figure 5

figure 6

figure 7

FOUND

INGENIOUS AND CREATIVE, a found wedding incorporates recycled, reused,
and vintage elements to craft a hip, eco-conscious celebration.

FOUND STYLE

PALETTES

Kraft paper   Blue   Green   Red   Yellow   White

INSPIRATION

Folk and outsider art, Margaret Kilgallen, Anthropologie store displays, vintage office and school supplies, vintage food packaging, flea markets, collecting, recycling, camping

FONTS

Archive Kludsky, Wade Vernacular Outline, Heroic Condensed Light, Bryant Regular, Register Serif, URW Underwood, Gill Sans Std, Remington Weather

TEXTURES

Kraft paper, newspaper, chipboard, chalkboard, corrugated cardboard, aluminum, glass, graph paper, loose-leaf paper, maps

VENUES

Gallery, beach, field, backyard, lodge, campground, community center

DETAILS

Use glassine pastry bags or kraft lunch bags for guest favors or welcome bags ✳ *Write your menu on a chalkboard* ✳ Use vintage or recycled fabrics to sew mix-and-match napkins ✳ *Use mix-and-match vintage office or folding chairs* ✳ If the wedding is outdoors, collect old plaid blankets for guests to use when it gets cool ✳ *Use an old mailbox, office mail pigeonhole, or library card catalog drawer to collect guest wishes* ✳ Collect wooden numbers for your table numbers, or use assorted found postcards ✳ *Design your own paper place mat with activities (connect the dots, word search, Mad Libs, etc.) relating to the bride and groom, and put a jar of crayons or colorful mini pencils at each place setting* ✳ Hire a band that includes a washboard player

PUTTING IT ALL TOGETHER

1.

BACKYARD FLOWERS

Choose common local flowers, such as sunflowers, daisies, or asters. If they're not literally growing in your backyard, pick them up at a local flower market or U-Pick flower farm.

2.

TIN CANS

Tin cans, washed and with their labels removed, make surprisingly elegant containers for centerpieces. Tie a bit of $1/8$-inch ribbon in your color palette around the can to create a polished look.

3.

CANDY BAR

In lieu of cake, set up a candy bar, featuring favorite vintage candies. Serve them in a variety of found dishes and jars, and rubber stamp glassine bags that guests can use to collect their favorites.

4.

KRAFT-PAPER LINENS

Use kraft paper rolls in lieu of a tablecloth or runner. Keep it simple, or stencil a pattern of plate, knife, and fork at each place setting (see page 117).

5.

COLLECTIBLE FAVORS

Use small collectibles, such as vintage matchbooks, Pez dispensers, bottle caps, novelty items, and ephemera, instead of favors. If desired, attach a tag to each to indicate the guest's table number.

6.

RECYCLED PAPER AND FABRICS

Recycled paper, from newspapers to magazines to scrapbooking paper to ticket stubs, can be used in countless ways throughout your wedding—for everything from pom-poms to covered lamp shades, to Découpage Votives & Vessels (page 219). Likewise, recycled fabric (old clothes, sheets, and curtains) can be handy for making a chuppah, ring pillows (see pages 45 and 183), Fabric-Wrapped Favors (see page 53), table runners (see page 155), or pennants (see page 223).

7.

VINTAGE ATTIRE

Wear a vintage wedding gown and veil, and outfit your bridesmaids in colorful vintage party dresses.

NORTH P

SARA & ANDREW WOODHOUSE
345 MOTT STREET, APT. 9
NEW YORK, NEW YORK 10012

TRACY
&
OWEN
115 FOURTH ST
APARTMENT 5C
BROOKLYN
NEW YORK
11215

ARLENE & ROGER UNDERWOOD
REQUEST THE PLEASURE OF YOUR COMPANY
AT THE MARRIAGE OF THEIR DAUGHTER

TRACY LOUISE
to
OWEN JOHN STEPHENS

SATURDAY, THE FOURTEENTH OF OCTOBER
TWO THOUSAND AND ELEVEN
AT HALF PAST FOUR IN THE AFTERNOON

Brooklyn Academy of Music
BROOKLYN, NEW YORK

POST.

TRACY + OWEN
115 FOURTH STREET, APT. 5C
BROOKLYN, NEW YORK
11215

ANCE, BELGIUM
THE NETHERLANDS
Ated and Drawn in the
National Geographic Society for
ational Geographic Magazine
MELVILLE BELL GROSVENOR, EDITOR

ATLAS PLATE 32 · JUNE 1960

NORTH
SEA

FOUND-PAPER INVITATIONS

Recycled and found papers become colorful envelopes for these otherwise-understated invitations. A bit of glassine, baker's twine, and a round label bring the ensemble together.

LEVEL
Easy

CATEGORY
Invitations

TIME
Printing—4 hours
Assembly—4 hours

WHEN TO START
12 weeks before
the wedding (Invitations
should be mailed 8 weeks
before the wedding.)

**GROUP OR
INDIVIDUAL**
Group (after printing)

- *Station 1: Trim the card and label stock.*
- *Station 2: Cut out the envelopes.*
- *Station 3: Make the envelopes.*
- *Station 4: Affix RSVP labels, guest address labels, and stamps.*
- *Station 5: Collate invitations and wrap in glassine.*
- *Station 6: Tie baker's twine and affix label.*
- *Station 7: Stuff and seal the envelopes.*

BUDGET
$250 (excluding postage)

MATERIALS
Makes 100 invitations
- One hundred twenty 8 1/2-×-11-inch sheets ecru or white cover stock for invitations (each sheet fits one invitations, plus overage)
- Thirty 8 1/2-×-11-inch sheets ecru or white cover stock for RSVP cards (each sheet fits four RSVP cards, plus overage)
- Twenty 8 1/2-×-11-inch sheets ecru or white label stock for RSVP labels (each sheet fits six address labels, plus overage)
- Forty 8 1/2-×-11-inch sheets ecru or white label stock for guest address labels (each sheet fits three address labels, plus overage)
- One 5 3/4-inch square envelope (optional if you are not using the envelope template provided)
- One hundred twenty-five 7-×-14 1/2-inch sheets of recycled maps, magazines, graph paper, or brown bags
- Sixty 12-×-12-inch sheets glassine (each sheet makes two wraps)
- One hundred 4-bar envelopes
- 50 yards baker's twine
- One hundred 1 1/2-inch round labels
- Postage stamps for RSVP and invitation envelopes (square envelopes require additional postage, so check with your post office or online, at www.usps.com, before purchasing stamps)

TOOLS
- Found Invitation templates (available online at www.chroniclebooks.com/handmade-weddings)
- Fonts: Gill Sans Std and Wade Vernacular Outline
- Laser or inkjet printer, with extra ink cartridges
- Craft knife, with extra blades
- Ruler
- Cutting mat
- Pencil
- Scissors
- Bone folder
- Glue sticks, or double-sided tape gun and extra tape (we recommend the 3M Scotch ATG 700 Transfer Tape Dispenser)
- Remoistenable envelope glue (optional)

Note: If you are assembling invitations with a group, be sure to have enough craft knives, rulers, cutting mats, and glue sticks to keep everyone busy—we recommend four to six of each.

HOW TO

1. Customize and print your invitations and labels.

Customize your invitations, RSVP cards, and RSVP and guest address labels using the online templates. Print 120 pieces of each on card stock and label stock, respectively. Using a craft knife, ruler, and cutting mat, cut the invitations, RSVP cards, and labels along the crop marks provided. As soon as your blade begins to dull, put in a fresh blade.

2. Make your envelopes.

Carefully pull apart your square envelope and open it so that it lays flat; this will be your template (if you are using the Envelope template provided online, skip this step and instead print the template on a sheet of 11-×-17-inch paper and cut it out). Place a sheet of recycled paper, wrong-side down, on your work surface and lay your envelope template on top of it. Trace around the envelope with a pencil. With a ruler and craft knife or scissors, cut out your envelope. With your recycled paper facing wrong-side up, fold the side flaps first, creasing with a bone folder for a sharp fold. Next, fold the bottom flap and crease. Unfold the bottom flap, and with a glue stick or tape gun, apply glue to the side flaps, and fold the bottom flap up over them, smoothing to adhere. Fold the top flap and crease. Repeat to make the rest of the envelopes. Once you are ready to mail your envelopes, use a glue stick to apply glue to the envelope flaps and seal them. Or apply envelope glue to the flaps and let them dry, to be remoistened when you are ready to mail.

3. Assemble the invitations.

Using a craft knife, ruler, and cutting mat, trim the glassine into 5 1/2-×-11 1/4-inch rectangles. Affix the RSVP labels to the 4-bar envelopes, and affix the guest labels to the square envelopes.

Remember to leave at least 1/2 inch clear at the bottom of each envelope for post office bar coding. Affix postage to the RSVP and invitation envelopes. Collate the invitations and RSVP cards.

Lay a piece of glassine on your work surface. Center the invitation set on top of it. Fold the sides toward the center of the invitation. Fold the bottom corners up to meet the center line, creating a triangular flap. Fold the flap to meet the center of the invitation. Repeat with the top corners.

Cut an 18-inch length of baker's twine. Center the twine on the invitation and wrap around the glassine, front to back. Tie a half-knot, and then wrap it back to front and tie another half-knot, as though you are tying a package. Center a round label over the half-knot and glassine flap and smooth it down. Trim the ends of the twine to about 1 inch. Insert the invitation set into an envelope so that when it is pulled out with your right hand, it is facing the right way up. Repeat to wrap the rest of the invitation sets. Seal the envelopes as desired.

VARIATIONS

The technique of making your own envelopes can be applied to many invitation styles by choosing different papers. You can also choose different types of ribbon or twine and labels to finish your invitations.

- **Girly Romantic:** Make your envelopes with pretty patterned wrapping paper, wallpaper, or 12- to 16-inch doilies. In lieu of a round label, use a wax seal.

- **Organic Minimal:** Use text-weight kraft paper, seed paper, or brown bags to make your envelopes. Wrap the invitations in white or natural cotton twine, and seal with a round khaki label. Rubber stamp a design or your initials on the label, if desired.

DÉCOUPAGE VOTIVES & VESSELS

LEVEL
Easy

CATEGORY
Décor

TIME
4 to 6 hours

WHEN TO START
1 to 2 weeks
before the wedding

GROUP OR INDIVIDUAL
Group
Get a group together with
a range of supplies, and
have each person make
her or his own votives.

BUDGET
$40 to $60

Found papers—such as vintage candy wrappers, book pages, maps, ledger sheets, and ticket stubs—give these simple glass votive holders pizzazz. Place three or four on each table, alongside your centerpieces, or apply the same technique to tin cans, vases, or jars for your flowers. Look for vessels and votives with straight sides, as these are easier to cover than fishbowl or flared shapes.

MATERIALS
Makes 48 votives
- Forty-eight 3-inch clear, straight votives
- Found papers, such as candy wrappers, ticket stubs, vintage maps, magazines, or book pages
- 48 votive candles

TOOLS
- Votive template (available online at www.chroniclebooks .com/handmade-weddings)
- Small paint brush
- Craft glue
- Scissors
- Paper punch (optional)
- Mod Podge in matte finish
- Medium-sized craft brush

HOW TO

1. Cover the votive holders with paper.

For small scraps, such as ticket stubs, brush glue onto the back of the paper and press onto the votives. For larger scraps, or to wrap a votive entirely in one paper, cut out the Votive template. Place the template over your paper scrap and cut around the outline with scissors. Brush glue on to the back of the paper and wrap it around the votive. If desired, layer papers over each other, or punch shapes out with a paper punch and layer on top of neutral papers. Cover all your votive holders as desired, and let them dry.

2. Cover the votive holders with Mod Podge.

Once the votives are dry, brush over all the papers with a coat of Mod Podge. This will provide a clear, uniform coating over your votive. Let dry thoroughly before placing the candles in the votives.

VARIATIONS

- **Organic Minimal:** Cover the votives with newspaper or butcher paper.

- **Modern Classic:** Cover the votives in patterned or striped decorative or wrapping papers.

FABRIC PENNANTS

LEVEL
Moderate

CATEGORY
Décor

TIME
6 to 7 hours

WHEN TO START
6 to 8 weeks
before the wedding

**GROUP OR
INDIVIDUAL**
Individual, or a small
group (for cutting)

BUDGET
$50 to $100, depending
on fabrics chosen

These fabric pennants are a simple, high-impact way to decorate everything from the wedding reception to a bridal shower or rehearsal dinner. Hang them across a tent, over a dance floor, along a wall behind a dessert bar, or along the edge of a bar or welcome table. The most time-intensive aspect of the project is cutting the fabric, so if you have spare tools (a cutting mat, rotary cutter, and ruler), enlist friends to help with this repetitive yet critical portion. Although a sewing machine makes this project light work, you can also use iron-on fabric adhesive for a similar effect. And if working with fabric seems daunting to you, never fear: colorful papers work well, too.

MATERIALS

Makes five 10-foot pennant strands

- One 8 1/2-×-11-inch sheet text-weight paper
- 1 yard each of 3 medium to lightweight coordinating fabrics, 55 inches wide
- 1 1/2 yards white lining fabric, or an old sheet (optional)
- 10 yards 1 1/2-inch twill tape
- Matching thread

TOOLS

- Pennant template (available online at www.chroniclebooks.com/handmade-weddings)
- Inkjet or laser printer
- Scissors
- Iron and ironing board
- 14-inch or longer ruler, ideally a clear quilter's ruler (we recommend Omnigrid)
- Large cutting mat, at least 18 × 24 inches
- Rotary cutter with fresh blades
- Sewing machine, or fusible bonding web or glue
- Straight pins

HOW TO

1. Make the Pennant template.

Print the Pennant template onto a sheet of 8 1/2-×-11-inch paper and cut out with scissors.

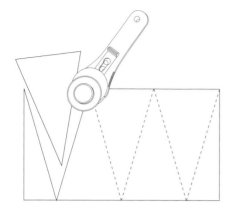

figure 1

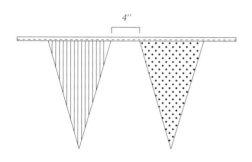

4"

figure 2

2. Cut out the pennants.

Iron the fabric to remove creases and wrinkles. Fold each yard of fabric into thirds, each section measuring 12 inches. Lay the fabric flat on your cutting mat. Using a rotary cutter, trim 1/4 to 1/2 inch from the top edge of the fabric, keeping a straight line. Align the top of the Pennant template to the newly trimmed edge. Using the rotary cutter, cut along the outline of the template (*figure 1*). Press firmly, as you are cutting through layers of fabric. Remove your first set of pennants. Turn the template upside down, and fit it into the angled area left behind by the first set of pennants. Cut along the flat bottom edge and angled left edge of the template to complete your second set of pennants. Repeat until all the fabric has been used. A 55-inch-wide yard of fabric should yield about 18 pennants.

3. Hem the pennants.

Place the pennant pairs back-to-back, mixing and matching the fabrics. If they are going to be strung across a room in daylight, hold them up to the light to make sure that the patterns do not show through. If the fabrics are too sheer, take some white lining fabric or an old sheet, and cut out additional pennants to sandwich between the two patterns, adding opacity.

Sew the two long sides of each pennant pair together using a zigzag stitch. If you are using fusible bonding web, cut two strips, each the length of one of the pennant's long sides. Sandwich each strip between the long edges of the pennants, and iron per the manufacturer's instructions.

4. Attach the twill tape.

Cut five 10-foot lengths of twill tape, adding extra length for hanging, as needed. (Feel free to adjust the length to your needs.) Lay each length on the ironing board, one by one. Fold it in half lengthwise, and iron flat. Starting at one end, use a running stitch (see page 35) to sew the twill tape in half for about 12 to 24 inches—more if you will need to tie the ends (such as around a column). If using fusible bonding web or glue, place the adhesive strip or dab glue inside the fold of the twill tape. Sandwich the straight side of the first pennant into the folded twill tape. Pin into place.

Note: If you place your pins perpendicular to the edge of your pennant, you can run the pennants right through the sewing machine, simply stitching over the pins. There is a small risk of hitting a pin and breaking your needle, so a bit of daring may be required, but it will save you time and ensure that your pennants stay in place as you sew.

Sew along the edge of the twill tape (approximately 1/16 inch in), or if using fusible bonding web, iron per the manufacturer's instructions. Continue to sew 4 inches of twill tape; then attach the next pennant *(figure 2)*.

VARIATIONS

This project can be made to fit just about any wedding with the right patterns and colors. For a beach wedding, choose neutral and sea foam or pale blue linens; for a winter wedding, choose woolens and plaids.

• **Organic Minimal:** Choose neutral fabrics, such as linen or burlap. Be imprecise when cutting the pennants, and consider using rectangles or squares instead of triangles for the pennants. To finish the pennants, use a straight running stitch, allowing the natural frayed edges to show.

• **Modern Classic:** Choose solid-colored fabrics or simple patterns, such as pinstripes, geometric forms, or monochromatic florals. Instead of twill tape, use satin or grosgrain ribbon.

• **Found:** Use found papers, such as old book or dictionary pages, newspaper, maps, or graph paper, mixed with festive solids. Or choose found or recycled fabrics from old sheets, shirts, dish towels, hankies, and the like.

• **Happy Graphic:** Use bright, graphically patterned paper or fabric combined with cheery solids. Consider alternating hearts and squares, instead of triangle shapes; instead of twill tape, use sturdy upholstery thread to sew a continuous strand through all the shapes.

jennifer + mark
april 16. 2011

PAPER-FLOWER WREATH

LEVEL
Moderate

. . . .

CATEGORY
Décor

. . . .

TIME
4 to 6 hours

. . . .

WHEN TO START
3 to 4 weeks
before the wedding

. . . .

GROUP OR
INDIVIDUAL
Group

. . .

- *Station 1: Cut out flower shapes.*
- *Station 2: Assemble flowers.*
- *Station 3: Wrap wreath form.*
- *Station 4: Assemble wreath.*

. . . .

BUDGET
$25 to $50

This lovely wreath uses a variety of found papers, including patterned paper scraps, kraft paper, glassine, tracing paper, and graph paper. Each flower center is made with a colorful brad.

MATERIALS
Makes 1 wreath
- 15 to 20 sheets assorted scrap papers (e.g., construction paper, kraft paper, graph paper, tissue paper)
- 30 to 40 colorful 1/4-inch brads
- Four 18-inch pieces floral wire (optional)
- One roll floral tape (optional)
- One 1 1/2-inch Styrofoam ball (optional)
- 1/4 yard scrap fabric
- 18-inch cardboard or particle-board wreath form
- Paper clip (optional)
- 1 to 2 pieces scrap cardboard or foam core
- 1 sheet text-weight paper (optional)

TOOLS
- Paper Flower templates (available online at www .chroniclebooks.com/ handmade-weddings)
- Pencil
- Scissors
- Small flower punches
- 1/8-inch hole punch
- Hot glue gun and glue sticks
- Inkjet printer, with extra ink cartridges (optional)

HOW TO
1. Make your flowers.
For flat flowers: Cut out the Paper Flower templates. Trace them onto patterned scrap paper, and cut out with scissors. Fold the flowers along the center axis of the petals to add dimension. You can also fringe the petals or crinkle flowers made of tissue to add depth. Punch small flower shapes for the flower centers. Stack several flower designs on top of each other, and punch a hole in the center. Insert a brad into the center and flatten the ends *(figure 1, page 228)*. Repeat to make as many flowers as desired.

figure 1

figure 2

figure 3

For cupped petal flowers: Cut out the Petal template. For each flower, trace the template four times onto graph paper or another text-weight paper. Cut the petals out. Slide a 6-inch length of floral wire into an unopened brad so that the brad grips firmly and the round end faces up. Fold the base of the petal into an M shape, position on the wire, and affix with a dab of hot glue. Place the next petal, and repeat until all four petals are in place. Wrap the petal bases with a strip of floral tape (*figure 2*). Repeat to make as many flowers as desired.

For tissue paper flowers: For each flower, cut four 1 1/2-×-4-inch strips of tracing paper or tissue paper. Place a piece of tissue, long side facing you, on your work surface. Center the Styrofoam ball on the paper, wrap the long ends up, and twist the ends to hold them in place. Trim the twisted ends with scissors and remove the ball, creating a cupped petal (*figure 3*). Repeat to create four petals per flower. Slide a 6-inch length of floral wire into an unopened brad so that the brad grips firmly and the round end faces up. Position a petal on the wire, and tape it in place with a strip of floral tape, wrapping it around the wire a few times. Place the next petal and repeat until all four petals are in place (*figure 4*). Repeat to make as many flowers as desired.

2. Prepare your wreath form.

Cut your scrap fabric into 3-inch-wide strips. Hot glue one end of a strip to the wreath form, and wrap it around the wreath until you run out of fabric (*figure 5*). Glue the fabric end down and continue with a new strip until the wreath is completely covered. Avoid covering the hole in the wreath (for hanging). If desired, flatten a paper clip into an S shape and insert it into the hole, to be used as a hook when you are ready to hang your wreath.

3. Attach your flowers.

Arrange your flowers in a wreath shape on your work surface. When you are happy with their placement, begin hot-gluing them to the form. To create depth, cut out several 1/2-inch squares of cardboard or foam core and affix these to the wreath form before gluing a flower on top, so that these flowers are slightly raised.

4. Add a sign (optional).

If desired, lay out a sign such as "Welcome!" or your names and wedding date using a word-processing program and printing on text-weight paper, or write the sign by hand. Attach to the wreath using a dab of hot glue.

VARIATIONS

- **Girly Romantic:** Make your flowers out of pretty shades of pink, lavender, and cream tissue paper. Write your sign in gold calligraphy ink.

- **Happy Graphic:** Choose bold, pop art–inspired papers.

- **Modern Classic:** Choose tailored patterned papers such as those used in the Punched-Paper Flower Centerpiece (see page 201).

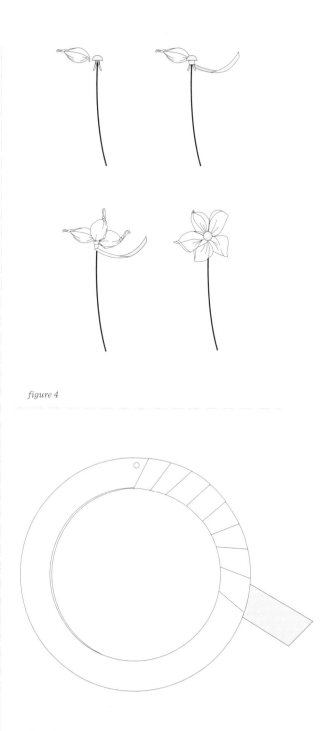

figure 4

figure 5

FABRIC-SCRAP HAIR CLIPS

LEVEL Easy	These sweet hair clips are perfect for flower girls, but they also add a lighthearted touch to bridesmaid attire. For best results, use two to three different fabrics and coordinating beads.

LEVEL
Easy

CATEGORY
Attire

TIME
4 to 6 hours

WHEN TO START
4 to 6 weeks
before the wedding

**GROUP OR
INDIVIDUAL**
Individual, or you
and a friend

BUDGET
Less than $10

These sweet hair clips are perfect for flower girls, but they also add a lighthearted touch to bridesmaid attire. For best results, use two to three different fabrics and coordinating beads.

MATERIALS

Makes 3 hair clips
- Fabric scraps, in two to three patterns
- Thread to match your fabric or beads
- 9 to 12 seed beads, or miniature pom-poms
- 3 hair clips or bobby pins

TOOLS

- 1-inch circle template
- Fabric pencil
- Fabric shears
- Sewing needle

HOW TO

1. Cut out the circles.

Lay the circle template over your fabric and trace with a fabric pencil. Trace five to six circles per hair clip. Cut them out with fabric shears, but don't worry about being precise; a slight variation in size adds to the aesthetic.

2. Attach the circles to the clips.

Thread the sewing needle, and knot the thread at one end. Neatly stack five to six circles, and sew one to two stitches through the center of the stack to secure it, ending with your needle on the right side. Thread a bead onto the needle and sew it down *(figure 1, page 232)*. Repeat with two more beads to create a small cluster, ending with your needle on the bottom side of the circles. Loop the thread through your clip or bobby pin. Make a stitch through the circles, and loop the needle back through the clip. Repeat until the circles are securely fastened to the clip *(figure 2, page 232)*. Repeat for each clip.

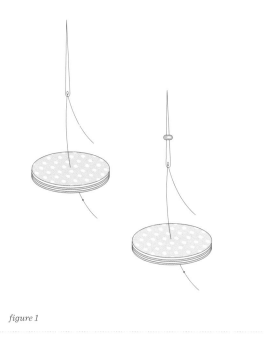

figure 1

figure 2

DRESS-PATTERN-&-FOUND-TISSUE BOUQUET

LEVEL
Moderate

CATEGORY
Ceremony

TIME
3 to 4 hours

WHEN TO START
3 to 4 weeks
before the wedding

GROUP OR INDIVIDUAL
Individual

BUDGET
$15 to $25

Vintage or new dress patterns, printed in black or blue on a yellowed tissue paper, are an excellent material for making paper flowers. Here, we combined them with recycled tissue papers to create peony-like blooms for a bridal bouquet. You can use the same technique to make pom-poms, boutonnieres, or corsages. If dress patterns aren't available, regular tissue paper (consider recycling pretty tissues from retail stores like Anthropologie) works well, too.

MATERIALS
Makes 1 bouquet
- 2 to 3 dress patterns, or 5 to 10 sheets tissue paper
- Fifteen to twenty 18-inch pieces cloth- or crepe paper–wrapped floral wire
- 1 sheet green tissue paper
- 2 yards 1½- to 2-inch twill tape

TOOLS
- Scissors
- Ruler, or tape measure
- Craft glue
- Floral tape
- Hot glue gun and glue sticks
- 2 to 3 corsage pins (optional)

HOW TO
1. Make the flowers.
For each flower, cut six identical rectangles from the dress pattern: six 8-×-12-inch sheets for a large flower, five 6-×-8-inch sheets for a medium-sized flower, and five 4-×-6-inch sheets for a small flower (we used a combination of medium-sized and small flowers). Stack the rectangles and fold them accordion-style along the short edge into 1-inch segments for large flowers, ³/4-inch segments for medium-size flowers, and ¹/2-inch segments for small flowers, resulting in a narrow rectangle *(figure 1, page 235)*. Using scissors, trim the ends of your rectangle *(figure 2, page 235)*: For rounded petals, like a

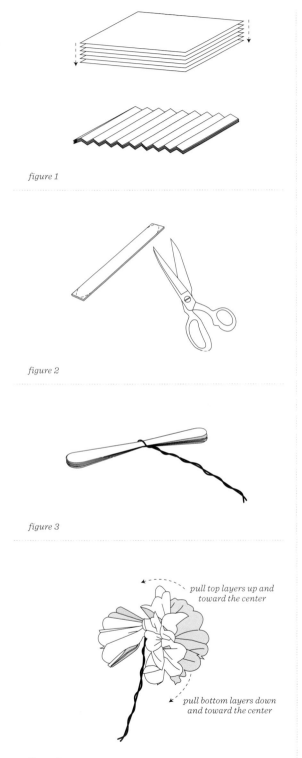

figure 1

figure 2

figure 3

pull top layers up and
toward the center

pull bottom layers down
and toward the center

figure 4

peony, cut each end into a scallop, or half-circle. For pointed petals, like a dahlia, trim the ends to a point. For a fringed flower, fringe the ends. Fold a piece of floral wire in half, slip it over the center of your rectangle, and tightly twist it (*figure 3*). Fan out the folds, and separate the layers of paper, one by one, pulling them toward the center and fluffing them out (*figure 4*). If desired, cup the petals and overlap them to make continuous concentric rings. Continue making flowers until you have a full bouquet, 10 to 15 flowers, depending on size.

2. Make the leaves.

For each leaf, cut two 3-×-5-inch paper rectangles, one out of green tissue paper and one out of an unprinted area of the dress pattern. Stack the rectangles and, using scissors, cut out a leaf shape. Apply craft glue to the top third of a piece of 9-inch floral wire. Sandwich the wire between the tissue paper leaves. Bend the wire slightly, and separate the layers of tissue to give the leaves dimension. Continue making leaves until you have enough to form a ring around the base of the bouquet.

3. Make the bouquet.

Arrange the flowers, surrounding them with a ring of leaves. When you are pleased with their appearance, twist the stems together, and tightly wrap floral tape around them to secure them. Wrap the taped stem in your twill tape. Fold 1 inch of the twill up over the end of your stem, and secure with a dot of glue. Wrap the long end around the fold and up the stem until you reach the top. Trim excess twill. Fold the loose end of the twill under and secure it with corsage pins or hot glue. Tie your remaining twill in a bow around the bouquet handle, letting the ends hang loose. Trim the ends at a 45-degree angle.

VARIATIONS

This technique can be used to make flowers out of tissue paper, too. Choose colors to match your wedding palette.

- **Modern Classic:** Choose a range of pink tissue papers, or make your bouquet out of white and cream tissue paper. Wrap the handle in white satin or black-and-white-striped grosgrain ribbon. If desired, decorate the entire length of the handle with a row of pearl-headed pins.

- **Girly Romantic:** Make your bouquet out of soft turquoise, pink, or lavender tissue paper, and wrap the handle with gold ribbon.

PEG-BOARD SEATING CHART

LEVEL
Easy

CATEGORY
Reception

TIME
4 to 6 hours

WHEN TO START
2 to 3 weeks
before the wedding

GROUP OR INDIVIDUAL
Group (after printing)

...

- *Station 1: Paint the Peg-Board.*
- *Station 2: Decorate the clothespins.*
- *Station 3: Trim the seating cards.*
- *Station 4: Attach the clothespins and seating cards.*

BUDGET
$75 to $100

Painted Peg-Board and clothespins decorated with patterned tape become an inexpensive, graphic seating chart in just a few simple steps. With such an eye-catching display, the seating cards themselves can be as simple as a typewriter font on plain paper. To conserve space, provide one seating card per couple.

MATERIALS

Makes one 3-×-4-foot seating chart with approximately 50 seating cards

- One 3-×-4-foot sheet Peg-Board (Peg-Board can be purchased in modular and custom sizes from your local hardware store or at Lowes, www.lowes.com. Adjust the size to fit the number of guests at your wedding. Each seating card requires approximately a 5-×-7-inch area of Peg-Board.)
- 1 pint white paint (optional, if Peg-Board is not prefinished)
- 1 roll kraft paper
- 50 wooden clothespins
- 6 to 10 rolls decorative tape in a variety of colors and patterns
- Ten 8 1/2-×-11-inch sheets white text-weight paper
- 1 roll thin nickel or copper wire

TOOLS

- Peg-Board Seating Card template (available online at www.chroniclebooks.com/handmade-weddings)
- Inkjet printer, with extra cartridges
- Font: Remington Weather
- 6 to 8 sheets newsprint (optional)
- Paint tray (optional)
- Paint roller (optional)
- Scissors
- Glue dots
- Craft knife
- Cutting mat
- Ruler
- Masking tape (optional)

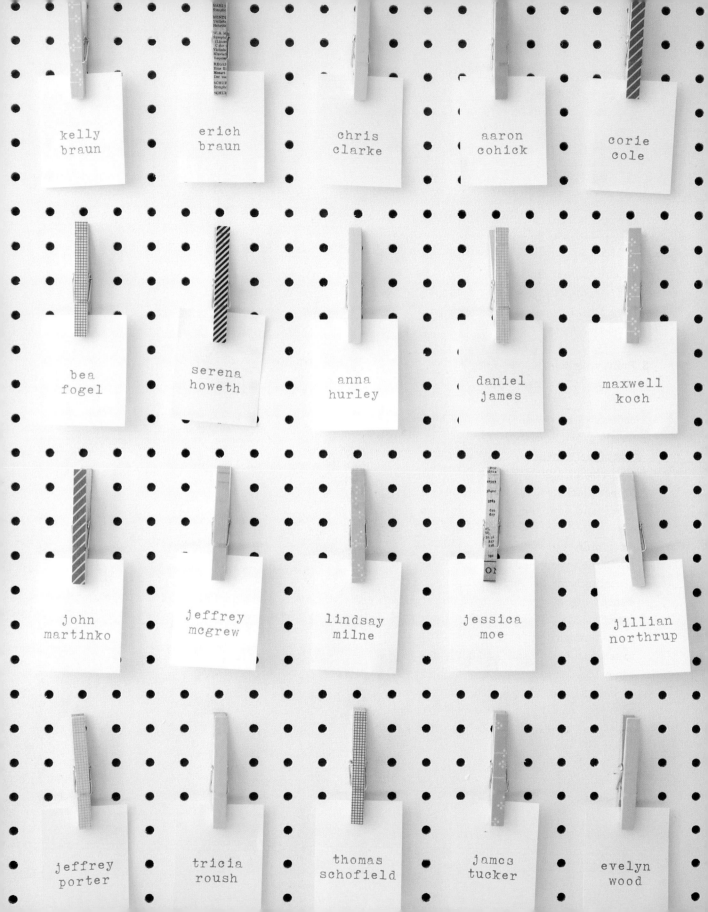

HOW TO

1. Prepare your Peg-Board.

Lay newsprint on the floor of your work area, and lean your Peg-Board against a wall or table on top of it. If using, roll a coat of paint onto the board. Let it dry. Apply another layer if desired.

Trim the kraft paper into panels that are sufficient to cover the back of your Peg-Board completely. Affix to the back of your Peg-Board with glue dots.

2. Decorate your clothespins.

Affix a strip of decorative tape along the length of each clothespin. Smooth it flat. Trim off any excess with a craft knife. Repeat on the other side.

3. Print your seating cards.

Using a word-processing program or the Peg-Board Seating Card template, customize your seating cards. Print them using an inkjet printer onto text-weight paper; because they are printed on both sides (guest's names on the front, table number on the back), print at least one test run to ensure proper alignment. Trim along the crop marks provided using a craft knife, ruler, and cutting mat.

4. Assemble your seating chart.

Decide how you would like to space your rows of seating cards. For each clothespin, thread an 8-inch length of wire through the spring (*figure 1*). Insert the wire ends into a hole in the Peg-Board, pierce through the kraft paper, twist a few times to secure the clothespin, and flatten the ends against the board, trimming with scissors if necessary (*figure 2*). If desired, secure the wire ends with masking tape (recommended if you are transporting the assembled board to your venue). Clip your seating cards to your clothespins in alphabetical order.

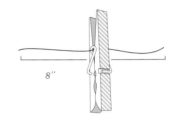

figure 1

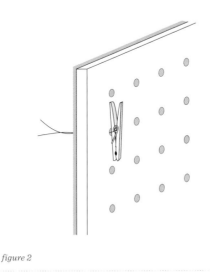

figure 2

VARIATIONS

- **Retro Homespun:** Paint the Peg-Board a cheery color, such as orange, and leave the clothespins in their natural state.

- **Happy Graphic:** Leave the Peg-Board unpainted, and decorate the clothespins in brightly colored tapes; or spray paint them vibrant colors such as red, blue, or yellow.

- **Organic Minimal:** Decorate the clothespins in neutral colors and minimal patterns, such as graph paper and wood grain.

CLIPBOARD MENUS

LEVEL
Moderate

....

CATEGORY
Reception

....

TIME
12 to 14 hours

....

WHEN TO START
2 to 3 weeks
before the wedding

....

**GROUP OR
INDIVIDUAL**
Group (after printing)

. . .

• *Station 1: Trace and trim the
patterned papers.*
• *Station 2: Affix the patterned
papers.*
• *Station 3: Trim the menus and
place cards.*
• *Station 4: Collate and attach
menus.*

....

BUDGET
$250 to $350, depending
on papers chosen

Simple 6-×-9-inch clipboards covered in patterned papers make charming holders for menus as well as place cards, photo-booth tickets, song-request cards, and more. Coordinating place mats made out of patterned paper or gift wrap finish the look.

MATERIALS

Makes 100 clipboards and menus
• One hundred 6-×-9-inch hard-
board clipboards
• 1 roll tracing paper (or one
hundred 8 1/2-×-11-inch sheets)
• 15 to 20 sheets patterned gift
wrap for covering clipboards
(calculate the quantity based
on the sheet size)
• 50 sheets patterned gift wrap
for place mats (optional)
• Eighty 8 1/2-×-11-inch sheets
text-weight paper (each sheet
fits two menus or four place
cards)

TOOLS

• Clipboard Menu and Place Card
templates (available online
at www.chroniclebooks.com/
handmade-weddings)
• Fonts: Gill Sans Std and Wade
Vernacular Outline
• Pencil
• Drafting tape
• Craft knife
• Ruler
• Cutting mat
• Glue sticks
• Bone folder
• Inkjet printer, with extra
ink cartridges

HOW TO

1. Cover the clipboards.

For each clipboard, use a pencil to trace the outline of the board and clip area onto tracing paper (because the clip placement sometimes varies, it's best to do them one at a time). Tracing the clip area can be tricky, so if you want to be precise, measure each angle and groove, and draw them out on your tracing paper.

Lay the tracing paper on top of your patterned paper, secure it with drafting tape, and cut it out using a craft knife, ruler, and cutting mat. Spread glue over the wrong side of the patterned paper, position it on your clipboard, and smooth it down with a bone folder.

If desired, cut 12-×-12-inch square place mats out of additional patterned paper.

2. **Print your menus and place cards.**
Customize your menus and place cards using the online templates and print on text-weight paper. Trim following the crop marks provided using a craft knife, ruler, and cutting mat. Clip the menus and place cards, if using , to your clipboards, along with any other ephemera you wish to include (e.g., wine-tasting notes, a personal note to each guest, a favor card noting a donation to a favorite charity, a song-request card, or a photo-booth ticket).

VARIATIONS

• **Happy Graphic:** Spray paint the clipboards red or another bright color (cover the clip area with masking tape first).

• **Organic Minimal:** Leave the clipboards in their natural state and dip the bottom 2 inches in chalkboard paint. Write each guest's name in chalk.

BRIDE & GROOM SHAKEYS

LEVEL
Easy

....

CATEGORY
Favors and gifts

....

TIME
4 to 6 hours

....

WHEN TO START
2 to 4 weeks
before the wedding

....

**GROUP OR
INDIVIDUAL**
Group

· · ·

- *Station 1: Cover the lids.*
- *Station 2: Attach the brides and grooms.*
- *Station 3: Fill the jars.*
- *Station 4: Seal the jars.*

....

BUDGET
$75 to $100

These shakeys (or snow globes) transform inexpensive bride and groom cake toppers into fun souvenirs for your guests. Collect an assortment of jam jars well in advance of your wedding, or, if they are in short supply, order from an online bottle and jar supplier.

MATERIALS

Makes 100 shakeys

- One hundred 3-×-4-inch jars
- 5 to 6 rolls decorative tape, or one hundred 5-×-5-inch sheets assorted found papers, such as origami paper, scrapbooking papers, security envelopes, or vintage maps
- One hundred 3-inch bride and groom cake toppers
- Water
- 1 bottle corn syrup
- 16 ounces white glass glitter (available at specialty craft suppliers such as German Corner LLC, www.german-usa.com)

TOOLS

- Goo Gone
- Craft knife
- Pencil
- Scissors
- Mod Podge in matte finish
- Medium-size craft brush
- Hot glue gun and glue sticks

HOW TO

1. Clean your jars.

Wash your jars thoroughly and remove any labels with Goo Gone. Let them dry.

2. Cover the lids.

With decorative tape: For each lid, starting at one end, affix several strips of tape across the lid, aligning the long edges to create a continuous layer of tape. Lay the lid tape-side down and trim excess tape

with a craft knife. Wrap a strip of tape around the edge of the lid, aligning one long edge to the top of the lid. Once the edge is completely covered, fold the excess tape over the bottom edge of the lid. Repeat for all lids.

With found papers: Lay a lid facedown on a piece of found paper. Trace a circle around the lid with a pencil. Then, trace a second circle approximately 1/4-inch larger than the lid plus the height. Cut out the larger circle with scissors. Cut radiating 1/4-inch strips from the outer edge to the inner circle. Using a craft brush, brush Mod Podge over the inner circle. Press the lid firmly down onto the glued area. Brush Mod Podge over the strips, two to three at a time. Fold them over the lip of the jar and press firmly. Make sure the strips end along the edge of the lid; if they extend to the center of the lid, trim down with scissors or a craft knife (the strips should not be visible once the lid is on). Brush the lid with a second coat of Mod Podge to seal it. Let it dry. Repeat for all lids.

3. Assemble the shakeys.

Hot glue a bride and groom cake topper to the inside of each lid. Let dry. Pour water into a jar until it is three-quarters full, and then add one teaspoon of corn syrup and one teaspoon of glitter. Top the jar off with water until it is filled to the brim. Screw a lid on tightly and shake. Make sure you are happy with the amount of glitter and the size of any air bubbles, and adjust the amount of water as needed. Remove the lid. Apply hot glue along the inside edge of the lid and, while it is still hot, screw the lid onto the jar. Let it dry. Repeat for all jars.

VARIATIONS

- **Retro Homespun:** Cover the lids in fabric.

- **Modern Classic:** Cover the lids in black paper. Add a circular label to the bottom of each lid, with a monogram or message to your guests.

APPENDIXES

TOOLS

Having the right tools is essential to happy crafting: minimizing frustration and tedium and making your projects look as polished and pretty as possible. Here are some of the tools we recommend having on hand.

. . . .

ADHESIVES

Craft glue
A water-based white glue that dries clear. It is non-toxic and can be cleaned up with soap and water.

Double-sided fusible web
Fusible web is made from a fabric that will melt when it is heated. Double-sided fusible web comes with a pressure-sensitive coating on both sides so you can adhere the web to your fabric, cut out your shapes, and then position and adhere them to another piece of fabric or paper. The fusible web stabilizes fabric so that you can work with it as you would paper.

Double-sided tape
Clear tape that is sticky on both sides, allowing you to attach papers together as you would with a glue stick.

Double-sided tape gun
A heavy-duty tape dispenser that allows you to efficiently adhere items together en masse. Great for lining envelopes or attaching backings to invitations. We recommend the 3M Scotch ATG 700 Transfer Tape Dispenser.

Drafting tape
An easily removable tape that does not leave a sticky residue when it is peeled off.

Glue stick
A solid adhesive in a twist or push-up tube. Great for working with paper, as the glue will not saturate the paper, causing it to wrinkle or curl.

Hot glue gun
An electric gun containing a heating element that melts a plastic glue that is sold in sticks. Creates a strong bond, and the glue dries within minutes.

Mod Podge
A paste glue that dries clear. It is nontoxic and can be cleaned up with soap and water.

Rubber cement
A latex-based glue that dries quickly and does not saturate or wrinkle the paper. Can be removed using an eraser without damaging the surface, if desired.

Spray adhesive
A glue that comes in a spray can. Excellent for applying a thin coat of glue that will not saturate your paper or cause it to wrinkle or curl. Also great for applying glue to delicate papers or larger items. Be sure to use in a well-ventilated area or outside. Also, it can get quite messy so make sure to protect your work surface.

Xyron machine
A tool for applying adhesive to the back of your paper. Whatever the shape of your paper, the machine applies glue only where there is a material present. Essentially, it allows you to make a sticker out of anything. Xyron machines (available at general craft stores) can be purchased in a variety of sizes, from 1 inch wide to $8 \frac{1}{2} \times 11$ inches.

CUTTING TOOLS

Awl

A small pointed tool (it looks a bit like a small ice pick) that can be used to punch small holes in papers. It can also be used as a substitute for a pencil when marking for cutting.

Circle cutter

An adjustable tool that allows you to cut perfect circles.

Corner rounder

A punch that rounds the corners of your paper.

Craft knife, or utility knife

A knife with a penlike body that holds a short, sharp, replaceable blade. Exceptionally handy for making quick, accurate cuts.

Tips:
- *Always have a fresh supply of blades on hand; dull blades will drag and create a ragged edge.*
- *Use a metal ruler when cutting with a craft knife; a metal ruler is more accurate and safer to use than a plastic ruler.*
- *When cutting through thick paper, make several shallow cuts rather than one deep cut—it will be easier on your cutting hand, and the resulting cut will be crisp and clean.*

Decorative paper punches

Punches are available in all sorts of shapes and sizes. You can get variations on the classic hole punch: punches for making shapes and corner rounders for cutting out fancy corners.

Decorative scissors

Decorative scissors have blades that will trim your paper with fancy edges, such as a scallop or zigzag.

Paper cutter

A trimmer that consists of a solid base, with marks to measure and align your paper, and either a rotary blade or guillotine blade. We recommend the type with a rotary blade, as you can easily replace the blade when it gets dull or swap it out for one with a decorative edge.

Rotary cutter

Typically used in sewing or quilting, this allows you to make clean, continuous cuts in fabric. The round blade allows you to apply a good amount of pressure, and the continuous motion of cutting minimizes snags.

FOLDING AND MEASURING TOOLS

Bone folder

A bookbinder's tool used to crease and smooth folds, score and burnish paper, and work materials into tight corners. It is polished to a smooth finish to avoid damaging the paper or fabric it is drawn across.

Cutting mat

A cutting mat is the best surface to use with a craft knife. The surface is self-healing and will protect the blade of the knife. It is also typically marked with a measuring grid that is handy for measuring and marking right angles.

Metal ruler

A metal ruler is safer and more accurate to use than a plastic ruler. It is available with a cork back to prevent slipping.

Quilting ruler

A wide see-through plastic ruler that is printed with a measuring grid, making it easy to measure, cut, and align paper or fabric.

Right-angle ruler

A handy tool for making right angles—especially useful for scoring and folding a card in half without having to do a lot of measuring and marking.

....

PAPER

Card stock

Heavyweight paper for making invitations, save-the-dates, menus, or place cards. Comes in a variety of colors and textures. Generally, it has a grain running in one direction, and it is easier to fold card stock with the grain. Always use a bone folder and ruler to get a clean fold.

Crepe paper

Flexible paper, stronger than tissue paper, that can be stretched along the grain and molded into shapes, such as flower petals. Comes in different weights. We recommend getting the heavy, German kind (sometimes double-sided), available from specialty craft boutiques such as www.castleintheair.biz.

Decorative paper

Can include wrapping paper, Japanese yuzen paper (decorative paper incorporating traditional kimono patterns), wallpaper, or origami paper. Great for lining envelopes, backing invitations, making paper cones, wrapping vessels, and the like. When shopping for decorative paper, keep in mind the scale of the pattern. Many wrapping papers have large-scale patterns that are not suitable to smaller items, such as an invitation.

Kraft paper

Looks like a brown bag, available in rolls (check the shipping department of drug or stationery stores) or in pads at some art supply stores.

Text-weight paper

Lightweight paper such as printer paper, résumé paper, or copy paper. Available from art supply and paper stores in a wide range of colors.

Tissue paper

Thin, porous paper available in a variety of colors. Great for making pom-poms and flowers.

Tracing paper

A type of paper (also known as onionskin) that is translucent, allowing you to see the image you want to trace though it.

....

RIBBONS AND TRIMS

Grosgrain ribbon

A heavy, ribbed ribbon, usually made of polyester or silk. Available in a wide range of colors and widths.

Satin ribbon

A sleek, medium-weight ribbon made of either silk or polyester. Available in a wide range of colors and sizes. Comes either single-faced (one shiny side, one matte side), or double-faced (both sides shiny).

Seam tape, or seam binding

A lightweight, inexpensive ribbon typically attached to the unfinished hem of fabric to keep it from unraveling. Available in a range of colors, it is excellent for embellishing stationery and favors.

Stitched ribbon

A decorative ribbon that has a running stitch, usually in a contrasting color, sewn along both edges.

Twill tape

A flat, twill-woven ribbon, typically made of cotton or linen. Has a natural, neutral, utilitarian look.

RESOURCES

Many thanks to the following vendors for loaning props and materials for our photo shoot:

Benjamin Moore
www.benjaminmoore.com
Paints

Betty Bakery
www.bettybakery.com
Cakes and sweets

Frances Palmer Pottery
www.francespalmerpottery.com
Cake stands

Hyman Hendler & Sons
www.hymanhendler.com
Vintage ribbon

Lulu DK
www.luludk.com
Wall covering

Middle Kingdom Porcelain
www.middlekingdomporcelain.com
Vases

Mokuba
www.mokuba.com
Ribbons

One Girl Cookie
www.onegirlcookie.com
Sweets and confections

Party Rental, Ltd.
www.partyrentalltd.com
Linens, tables, and chairs

Pikku Wares
www.pikkuwares.com
Patterned papers

Rowenta
www.rowenta.com
Professional irons

Sonia's Place
www.designtrade.net
Wall covering

RETRO HOMESPUN

Bake It Pretty
www.bakeitpretty.com
Cupcake liners

B&J Fabrics
www.bandjfabrics.com
Fabric

Clotilde
www.clotilde.com
Sewing supplies

Fancy Flours
www.fancyflours.com
Cupcake liners

Fat Quarter Shop
www.fatquartershop.com
Fabric

ImagiKnit
www.imagiknit.com
Yarn, twine-like yarn

Layer Cake Shop
www.layercakeshop.com
Cupcake liners

M&J Trimming
www.mjtrim.com
Buttons, ribbons, and trims

Michaels
www.michaels.com
Embroidery hoops and thread

Paper Source
www.paper-source.com
Colored paper and envelopes

Purl Soho
www.purlsoho.com
Wool felt, fabric

Super Buzzy
www.superbuzzy.com
Fabric

. . . .

GIRLY ROMANTIC

B&J Fabrics
www.bandjfabrics.com
Fabric

Bell'occhio
www.bellocchio.com
Decorative papers, ribbons, and trims

Blick Art Materials
www.dickblick.com
Gold paint pen

Britex Fabrics
www.britexfabrics.com
Fabric, interfacing

City Stamp + Sign
www.stampnsign.com
Custom rubber stamps

Coffee Wholesale USA
www.cw-usa.com
Bulk commercial coffee filters

General Bead
www.genbead.com
Picture frame charms, beads, and buttons

Jo-Ann Fabrics
www.joann.com
Sewing supplies and interfacing

Judith M. Millinery Supply
www.judithm.com
Buckram, veiling, and millinery wire

Martha Stewart Crafts
www.marthastewartcrafts.com
Decorative papers

Masterstroke
www.masterstrokecanada.com
Ribbons

Mistral Soap
www.mistralsoap.com
French milled soap

Mokuba
www.mokuba.com
Ribbons

Paper Mojo
www.papermojo.com
Decorative papers

Paper Source
www.paper-source.com
Heat embossing tool, embossing powder,
rubber stamp pads, and decorative paper

The Ribbonerie
www.theribbonerie.com
Ribbons

Rubber Stamps, Inc.
www.rubberstampsinc.com
Custom rubber stamps

Sierra Enterprises
www.sierra-enterprises.com
Rubber stamp pads

Sugarcraft
www.sugarcraft.com
Cake boards

. . . .

HAPPY GRAPHIC

Blick Art Materials
www.dickblick.com
Hinge clamps for silk-screening;
home screen-printing kits

City Stamp + Sign
www.stampnsign.com
Custom rubber stamps

Creative Wholesale
www.creative-wholesale.com
Wavy fan handles

Dafont
www.dafont.com
Free downloadable fonts

Dr. Don's Buttons
www.buttonsonline.com
Button-making supplies

Etsy
www.etsy.com
Suggested sellers:
• www.etsy.com/shop/goosegrease
• www.etsy.com/shop/gemmielou
Male and female wood dolls

EZ Screen Print
www.ezscreenprint.com
Photo EZ screen-printing kit,
an alternative to having screens
professionally made

Fishs Eddy
www.fishseddy.com
Glass water bottles

Frank Edmunds & Company
www.frankedmunds.thomasnet.com
Butter knife fan handles

General Bead
www.genbead.com
Seed beads and decorative buttons

Hello!Lucky
www.hellolucky.com
Patterned papers

The Hobby Co. of San Francisco
www.hobbycosf.com
Styrofoam discs

Myfonts.com
www.myfonts.com
Downloadable fonts

The Packaging Store
www.the-packaging-store.com
Kraft boxes

Paper Source
www.paper-source.com
Envelopes

Papier Valise
www.papiervalise.com
Heart-shaped brads, ephemera,
and notions

Pikku Wares
www.pikkuwares.com
Patterned papers

POP The Soda Shop
www.popsoda.com
All kinds of soda pop

Rubber Stamps, Inc.
www.rubberstampsinc.com
Custom rubber stamps

Standard Screen Supply Corporation
www.standardscreen.com
Custom silk screens and silk-
screening supplies

U.S. Box
www.usbox.com
Resealable kraft coffee bags

Utrecht
www.utrechtart.com
Borden & Riley #840 Kraft Pad

Vinyl-Decals.com
www.vinyl-decals.com
Vinyl decals

. . . .

ORGANIC MINIMAL

Blick Art Materials
www.dickblick.com
Jumbo craft sticks, balsa wood,
chalkboard spray paint, Mastercarve
artist's carving block, and linoleum
block–carving tools

California Paper Goods
www.capaper.com
Mini clothespins

Celestial Gifts
www.celestialgifts.com
Muslin bags

City Stamp + Sign
www.stampnsign.com
Custom rubber stamps

Lake Charles Manufacturing
www.testtubesonline.com
Test tubes

Paper Source
www.paper-source.com
#10 top-opening envelopes, eyelets,
eyelet setter, $\frac{1}{4}$-inch brads

Paperworks
www.paperworks.com
Greengrocer Brown Bag Paper

Pikku Wares
www.pikkuwares.com
Patterned papers

Rubber Stamps, Inc.
www.rubberstampsinc.com
Custom rubber stamps

Save on Crafts
www.save-on-crafts.com
Fishbowl vases and Texas tallow berries

Smock
www.smockpaper.com
Patterned papers

. . . .

MODERN CLASSIC

Castle in the Air
www.castleintheair.biz
Crepe paper, floral wire, decorative
paper, and calligraphy supplies

Clotilde
www.clotilde.com
Mega Pleater, point turner, and
sewing supplies

D. Blumchen & Company
www.blumchen.com
Crepe paper, floral pips, decorative
paper, and notions and trims

Hello!Lucky
www.hellolucky.com
Patterned papers

The Hobby Co. of San Francisco
www.hobbycosf.com
Styrofoam discs

Hollander's
www.hollanders.com
Book cloth (Japanese book cloth)

Hyman Hendler & Sons
www.hymanhendler.com
Vintage ribbons

Jennifer Osner Antique Textiles
www.jenniferosner.com
Vintage ribbons

JKM Ribbons & Trims
www.jkmribbon.com
Ribbons

Jo-Ann Fabrics
www.joann.com
Dritz Fray Check and sewing supplies

Mokuba
www.mokuba.com
Ribbons

Olde English Crackers
www.oldenglishcrackers.com
Christmas cracker snaps

Paper Mart
www.papermart.com
Colored tissue paper

The Ribbonerie
www.theribbonerie.com
Ribbons

Save on Crafts
www.save-on-crafts.com
Bleached Japanese Mitsumata branches

Tinsel Trading Company
www.tinseltrading.com
Vintage ribbons and notions

. . . .

FOUND

Anvente Event Essentials
www.weddingflowersandmore.com
Bride and groom cake toppers

Bake It Pretty
www.bakeitpretty.com
Baker's twine

B&J Fabrics
www.bandjfabrics.com
Fabric

Container and Packaging Supply
www.containerandpackaging.com
Glass jars

Create for Less
www.createforless.com
Styrofoam balls, floral wire, and
floral tape

Etsy
www.etsy.com
Vintage papers and ephemera

Fat Quarter Shop
www.fatquartershop.com
Fabric

German Corner LLC
www.german-usa.com
Glass glitter

MFG Direct
www.mfgdirect.com
Clipboards

Michaels
www.michaels.com
Particleboard wreath form

Nothing Elegant
www.etsy.com/shop/nothingelegant
Decorative tape

Paper Source
www.paper-source.com
Round labels, paper, and envelopes

Pikku Wares
www.pikkuwares.com
Patterned papers

Save on Crafts
www.save-on-crafts.com
Glass votives

Super Buzzy
www.superbuzzy.com
Fabric

Twilltape.com
www.twilltape.com
Twill tape

WEDDING PLANNING TIME LINE

Good advance planning is crucial to a relaxed and joyful wedding day, especially if you're planning to incorporate handmade details. Use the checklist below as a starting point. If you have less than a year or even six months to plan your wedding, don't worry. Just focus on the most essential elements first, and add personalized details as time allows.

12 TO 16 MONTHS AHEAD

- Pick a wedding date. Keep in mind the season and regional weather conditions, particularly if you are planning an outdoor wedding.
- Start a wedding file. This is where you'll keep your ideas, inspiration, potential DIY projects, contracts, and time lines. Begin scouring magazines, blogs, and other resources for inspiration.
- Decide on the style, size, and level of formality of your wedding. Be sure to discuss with family members who are going to be involved in planning and contributing to wedding costs.
- Start a rough guest list. Remember you'll need to combine your list with his list, as well as those of your parents. If the number of guests you can invite is limited by your venue or budget, give each set of parents a fixed number of guests they may invite in advance, and try to keep that number even on both sides. We recommend using a spreadsheet program that allows online collaboration, such as Google Docs, so multiple people can edit the list.
- Decide on a wedding budget. Adjust your guest list, time of year, or venue ideas accordingly. Be sure to factor in at least 10 percent extra for inevitable hidden costs.
- Hire a wedding planner, if desired. It's a good idea to do this early in the process, as the planner can help you pick a venue, home in on your style, and identify vendors.
- Select a ceremony venue and reception site that fit your style, guest count, and time of year. These will often be the same location but if they're not, be sure that both venues are available on your wedding date. Put down a deposit to reserve the date. Take photos for planning and styling purposes, get a floor plan and measurements, and find out if there are any limitations on hanging décor and signage. Confirm set-up and break-down times, and book extra time for set-up if you'll need it.

8 TO 12 MONTHS AHEAD

- Order a wedding gown. Remember that fittings and alterations take time, and custom gowns are not refundable so it pays to shop for one you love. Also look for matching accessories such as a veil and shoes.
- Choose attendants and request their participation. Begin shopping for attendant attire so they have plenty of time to order custom items if needed.
- Refine your style and color palette.
- Make a list of DIY projects and a DIY time line, and begin sourcing materials.
- Identify your DIY crafting team—this is your core group of friends or bridesmaids who will be helping you with craft projects. Get started on some of the larger or more time-consuming projects.

- Continue to compile and refine your guest list, and organize/verify addresses.
- Book a caterer. Often the caterer is dictated by the venue, but if they are not, interview several candidates and attend tastings. Do not scrimp here: the caterer calls the shots behind the scenes at the wedding reception (they control the timing of food and beverage service), so be sure to evaluate their efficiency and organizational skills along with the food.
- Book a photographer. This is perhaps the most important vendor, since they will determine how the wedding is remembered. Evaluate portfolios, but also be sure to meet with candidates personally to make sure you feel at ease around them. You can also book the photographer for an engagement photo shoot at this time. This is a great way to get comfortable with the photographer, and you can also use these photos for your save-the-date cards, if desired.
- Book a florist. Review portfolios, and look for someone whose personality is a good fit with yours and who will be open to your style suggestions and to incorporating your DIY ideas. Flowers are a big (and expensive) part of the wedding décor, so spend time doing your research.
- Book music for the ceremony and reception. Remember that the ceremony, cocktail hour, and dinner reception are all distinct portions of the event and may call for different music or musicians. If budget allows, hire a live band or professional DJ for at least part of the reception. While it can be fine to "iPod DJ" a portion of your wedding (say the ceremony or the after-party), remember that you still need a professional sound system and someone to manage the iPod. Mix songs in advance to ensure a good variety, and remove long lead-ins, codas, and awkward silences.
- Book a lighting designer. An oft-overlooked element of the wedding, lighting sets the mood, particularly if you are having an outdoor or tented wedding. The lighting designer can also coordinate "pipe-and-drape," e.g., fabric draping that can create distinct areas in your reception, such as a lounge area, or cover up unsightly wall hangings or fixtures.
- Throw an engagement party (or have friends or family throw one for you). This is a great way for everyone to start getting to know each other, so they'll have more fun on your wedding day!

6 TO 8 MONTHS AHEAD

- Make or order and mail out save-the-date cards, if using. Set up a wedding Web site, if using, and reserve hotel-room blocks for out-of-town guests.
- Start working on DIY projects, beginning with those that are either time consuming or require multiples (e.g., pom-poms or garlands, votives, drink flags) and/or those that aren't dependent on knowing a final guest count (e.g., ring pillow, flower girl garland or headband, bridal party accessories).
- Order a wedding cake.
- Book an officiant. Interview a few, and consider friends and family members. Choose one who fits your beliefs, style, and the tone of your wedding.
- Plan and book your honeymoon.
- Sign up for a gift registry. We recommend using a registry service like www.myregistry.com, which allows you to add items for any retailer on the Web, as well as register for cash gifts.

4 TO 6 MONTHS AHEAD

• Reserve rental equipment, such as tents, tables, chairs, linens, dinnerware, glassware, and portable restrooms, if needed. *Note: It is often best to leave rentals to the caterer, since they know what quantities they will need and can coordinate drop-off and pick-up times that work for them.*

• Decide on favors and begin making and assembling them (if they are not perishable).

• Book a makeup artist/hair stylist.

• Book transportation/limousine service for the wedding party and guests to and from the reception. Book or decide on a getaway car, if using.

• Purchase wedding rings.

• Purchase or reserve groom's attire. Make any special accents for the groom and groomsmen, such as pocket squares.

• Book a room for the wedding night.

• Sign up for dance lessons and decide on your first dance.

2 TO 4 MONTHS AHEAD

• Make or order and mail out your invitations. Book a calligrapher, or if you're planning to learn calligraphy yourself, start practicing! Remember to check the post office for the latest postage rates. Invitations should be mailed eight weeks before the wedding, ten to twelve weeks if you are expecting a lot of out-of-town guests and have not already mailed save-the-date cards. If you have a lot of out-of-town guests, consider asking them to note their arrival and departure dates and where they are staying on the RSVP card.

• Finalize details of the menu with the caterer. Confirm arrival and departure times, and rentals. Decide on server attire (e.g., bistro aprons, striped shirts), if desired.

• Plan the ceremony. Discuss the order of service with your officiant. Choose readings and music. Write your wedding vows, if desired, or confirm the traditional vows you will be using.

• Schedule a rehearsal time and rehearsal dinner (traditionally hosted by the groom's family).

• Meet with your makeup artist to try out the makeup and hair style.

• Buy stockings or any special lingerie for your dress and honeymoon.

• Choose your wedding music. Share your list with your DJ or band, or mix your iPod playlist and book sound equipment.

1 TO 2 MONTHS AHEAD

• Make a detailed event time line, including load-in, set-up, arrival, and departure times of all vendors; drop off of welcome bags to guest rooms; shuttle pickups; guest arrival times; ceremony start time; order and timing of toasts; first dance; cake cutting; and shuttle departures.

This is where a wedding planner comes in very handy! If you do not have a wedding planner, designate two or three attendants to be the day-of coordinators/"cruise ship directors." Make sure they have each other's cell phone numbers. Share this time line with all vendors.

- Make or order programs.
- Make or order a guest book.
- Make or order menus, if needed.
- Make or order a cake topper.
- Make arrangements for pre-wedding events, such as welcome cocktails, and a post-wedding brunch, if desired.
- If your state requires a blood test to obtain a marriage license, visit your physician.
- Obtain a marriage license and certified copies.
- Send change-of-address information to the post office, if needed.
- Contact local newspapers about publishing a wedding announcement, if desired.

TWO WEEKS AHEAD

- Follow up with guests who have not yet RSVP'ed.
- Begin making a seating plan, write seating cards and/or place cards, and make table numbers.
- Make additional signage, such as bar or buffet signs, reserved seating signs, bride and groom's seating signs, a guest-book sign, and a "Just Married!" sign.
- Write guest welcome letters, if using.
- Notify caterer of guest count.
- Write toasts for rehearsal dinner and wedding reception.
- Confirm where out-of-town guests are staying, and when they are arriving.

ONE WEEK AHEAD

- Finalize seating plan and update seating cards and place cards.
- Make guest welcome bags, if using. Deliver to guest rooms in conjunction with guest check-in dates.
- Circulate finalized event time line to all vendors and vendor contact list (include cell phone numbers of attendants who will be helping with specific tasks).
- Assign specific responsibilities to attendants, e.g., handing out programs, handing out corsages and boutonnieres, hanging signs, delivering welcome bags, coordinating timing of toasts and the first dance with the DJ, etc.
- Confirm rehearsal plans with attendants.
- Pack for your honeymoon and gather all necessary travel documents.
- Organize your wedding-day attire and accessories. Pack an emergency kit including: Band-Aids, bobby pins, cell phone, club soda (for stain removal), deodorant, double-stick tape (for fallen hems), extra stockings, ibuprofen, makeup and makeup remover, nail polish and nail-polish remover, prescription medications, safety pins, sewing kit, snacks, tampons/pads, tissues, toothpaste and toothbrush, and water.

ONE DAY AHEAD

- Set up ceremony and reception décor, including lighting. Receive deliveries.
- Confirm transportation arrangements.
- Rehearse ceremony and attend rehearsal dinner.
- Give gifts to the wedding party.
- Prepare tip and payment envelopes for officiant and vendors; arrange for someone to distribute them.
- Have a manicure and pedicure, and a massage!

YOUR WEDDING DAY

- Have your attendants take care of last-minute details, such as setting out place cards, seating cards, and programs.
- Give the wedding rings to the best man.
- Relax, and have fun!

HOW TO ADDRESS AND ASSEMBLE YOUR INVITATIONS

ADDRESSING YOUR INVITATIONS

Use the table on opposite page as a general guideline for how to address your guests by guest type. In addition, follow these simple rules of thumb:

Spell out guest names exactly as you want them to appear:
- Titles (e.g., Mr., Ms., Mrs., Doctor, Reverend, The Honorable)
- Add "and guest" where applicable
- Add children's names or "and family" where applicable

Spell out all abbreviations:
- State names
- Words like Street, Road, Avenue, Boulevard, Circle, etc.
- Directions (e.g., North, South, East, West)
- Apartment (# or No. are acceptable in a pinch)

Double-check the correct formatting of international addresses:
- Sometimes the zip code comes before the state or country

Guest Type	Salutation
Married Couple	Mr. and Mrs. John Gilbert
With children under 18 living at home	Mr. and Mrs. John Gilbert Heather and Michael Gilbert *or* Mr. and Mrs. John Gilbert and family
In which the woman kept her maiden name	Ms. Christine Brown and Mr. John Gilbert
In which the man is a doctor	Doctor and Mrs. John Gilbert
In which both are doctors	Doctor Christine Brown and Doctor John Gilbert
In which the woman is a doctor	Doctor Christine Brown and Mr. John Gilbert
Single Woman	Ms. Christine Brown Gilbert or Miss Christine Brown Gilbert
Single Man	Mr. John Gilbert
Guests	If a guest is invited, it is appropriate to add "and guest" to the envelope
Unmarried Couple Living Together	Miss Christine Brown Mr. John Gilbert
Divorced Woman	
Using married name	Ms. Christine Brown Gilbert *or* Mrs. Christine Brown Gilbert
Using maiden name	Ms. Christine Brown
Widow	Mrs. John Gilbert

ASSEMBLING YOUR INVITATIONS

Although you are welcome to use creative license when deciding how to present your invitations, you should be aware of the following traditional rules of thumb:

• Invitation and enclosures are placed in the envelope so that they are facing right-side up when pulled out with your right hand.

• The enclosures are stacked from largest to smallest, with the RSVP set placed on top of the invitation. If there are two cards of the same size (e.g., the invitation and a map or directions card), place the more important card on top.

• The RSVP card is tucked under the flap of the stamped RSVP envelope, not placed inside it. Remember, no postage is needed for RSVP cards that will be mailed back to you from out of country (because respondents must supply their own postage).

TIPS FOR ASSEMBLING AND MAILING INVITATIONS

• Number your RSVP cards lightly in pencil on the backside, and match these numbers up to your guest list. This way, if a respondent accidentally omits his or her name or that of a guest, you can follow up appropriately.

• Use an envelope moistener with adhesive to seal your envelopes securely. This is an especially good idea if you are using a thick card stock, such as chipboard, or have three-dimensional elements to your invitation, such as buttons or ribbon.

• Remember that invitations with a three-dimensional component and square invitations are subject to a non-machinable surcharge. Check with your post office or online, at www.usps .com, for rates.

INDEX